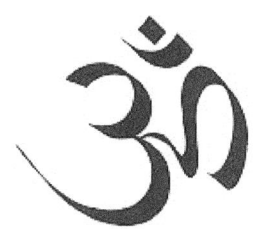

Rangoli Patterns

C R Patel

What is Rangoli?

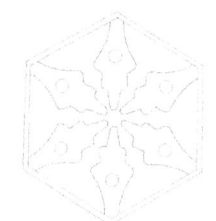

Rangoli is a popular art-form that consists of drawing images and motifs on the floor and using powders of different colors. The art of rangoli is known by different names in different parts of India such as Alpana (in Bengal), and Kolam (in South India). The significance of Rangoli is to welcome the Goddess Laxmi, the Goddess of wealth, into an individual's home and thus the rangoli stands for a sign of welcome. Rangolis are usually drawn on the doorstep for this reason.

How do you make a Rangoli?

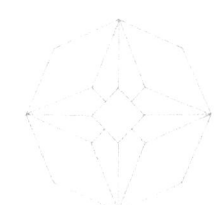

A rangoli is an art form and will reflect the creativity, personality and skill of the creator. To make a rangoli, powder is grasped between the thumb and forefinger in a pinch, and gently placed in its place. Lines are drawn with one finger movement and no unbroken lines are left. The spaces are then filled in with colored powders. Care in placement and design will result in the perfect rangoli. The process may be long, laborious and time-consuming, but the results are worth it as you see a vibrant and colorful design unfold in front of your eyes.

What can you use to make a Rangoli?

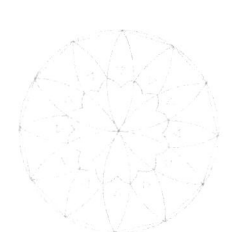

Many different items can be used to make a Rangoli. Traditionally, colored powder is used to form the rangoli on a floor. The powder can consist of finely ground rice flour, crushed limestone, or powdered chalk. The colors can be derived from natural products such as the tree leaves and barks, food products such as red chilies or tumeric or food coloring pastes or drops. Colored sand can also be used for the rangoli. Other readily available materials such as cereals, seeds, pulses, flowers, flower petals, or leaves can also be used.

Why should we make a Rangoli?

Rangoli is an art form that complements the joyous celebrations and festivities of Diwali. A rangoli reflects Indian culture and traditions as well as individual creativity, and upholds the timeless values of hospitality and reverence for divine beings.

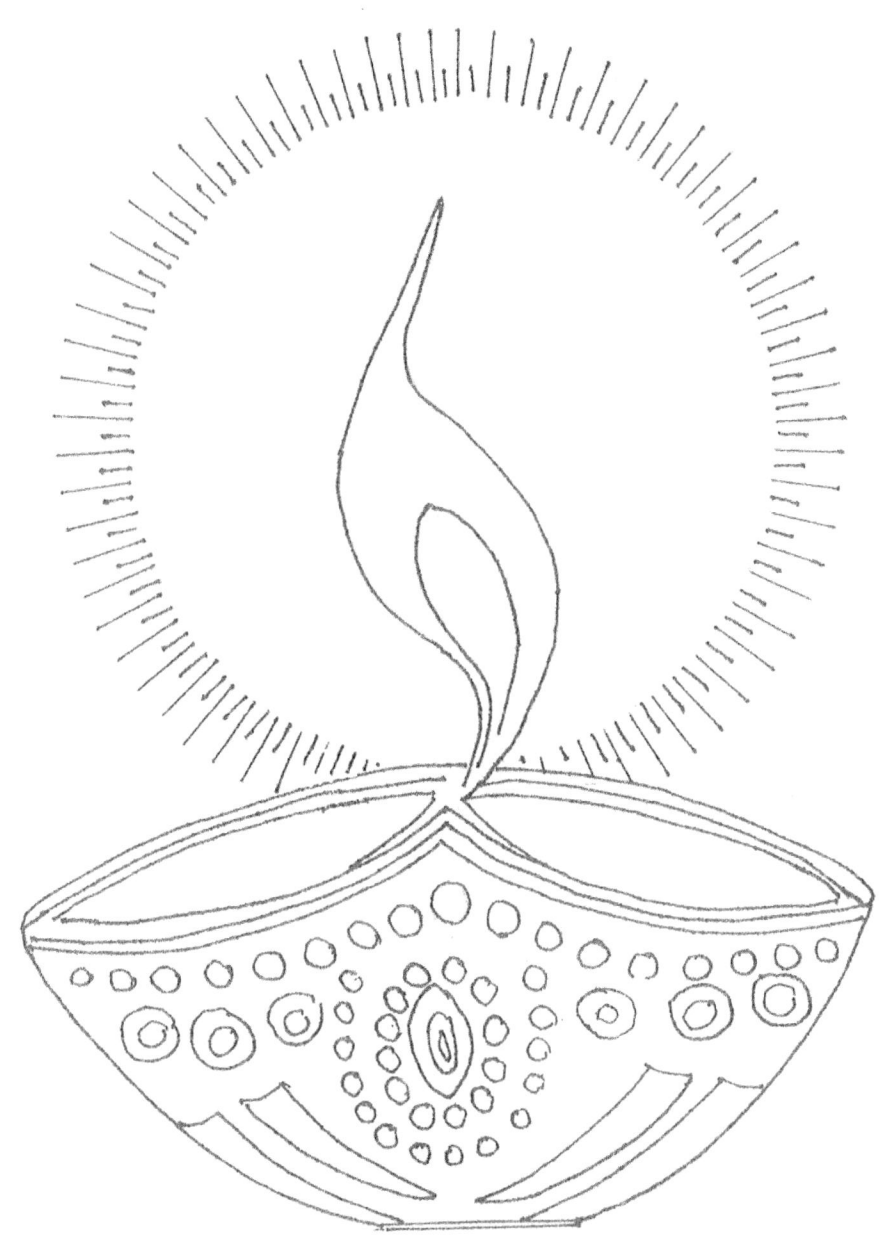

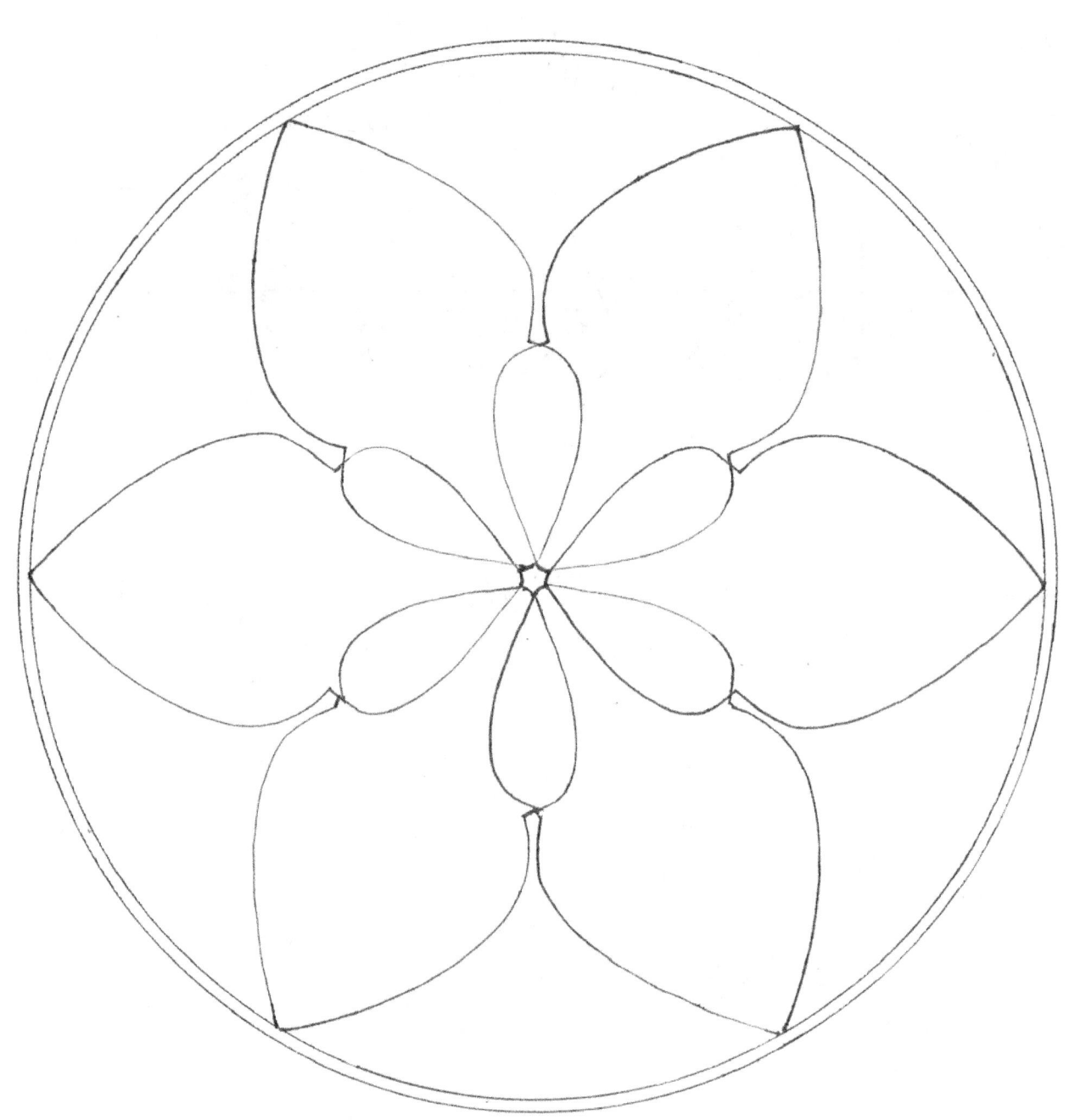

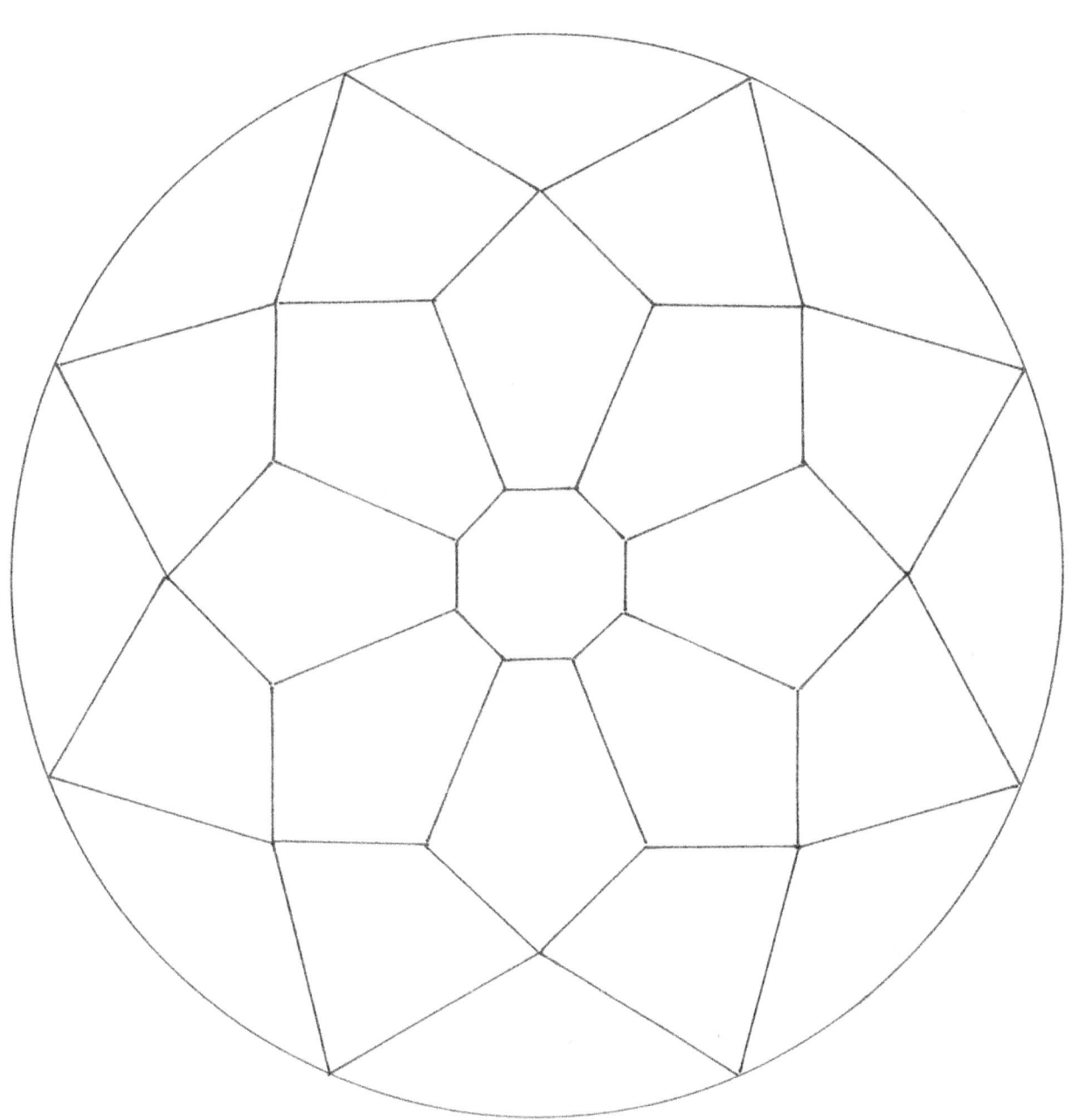

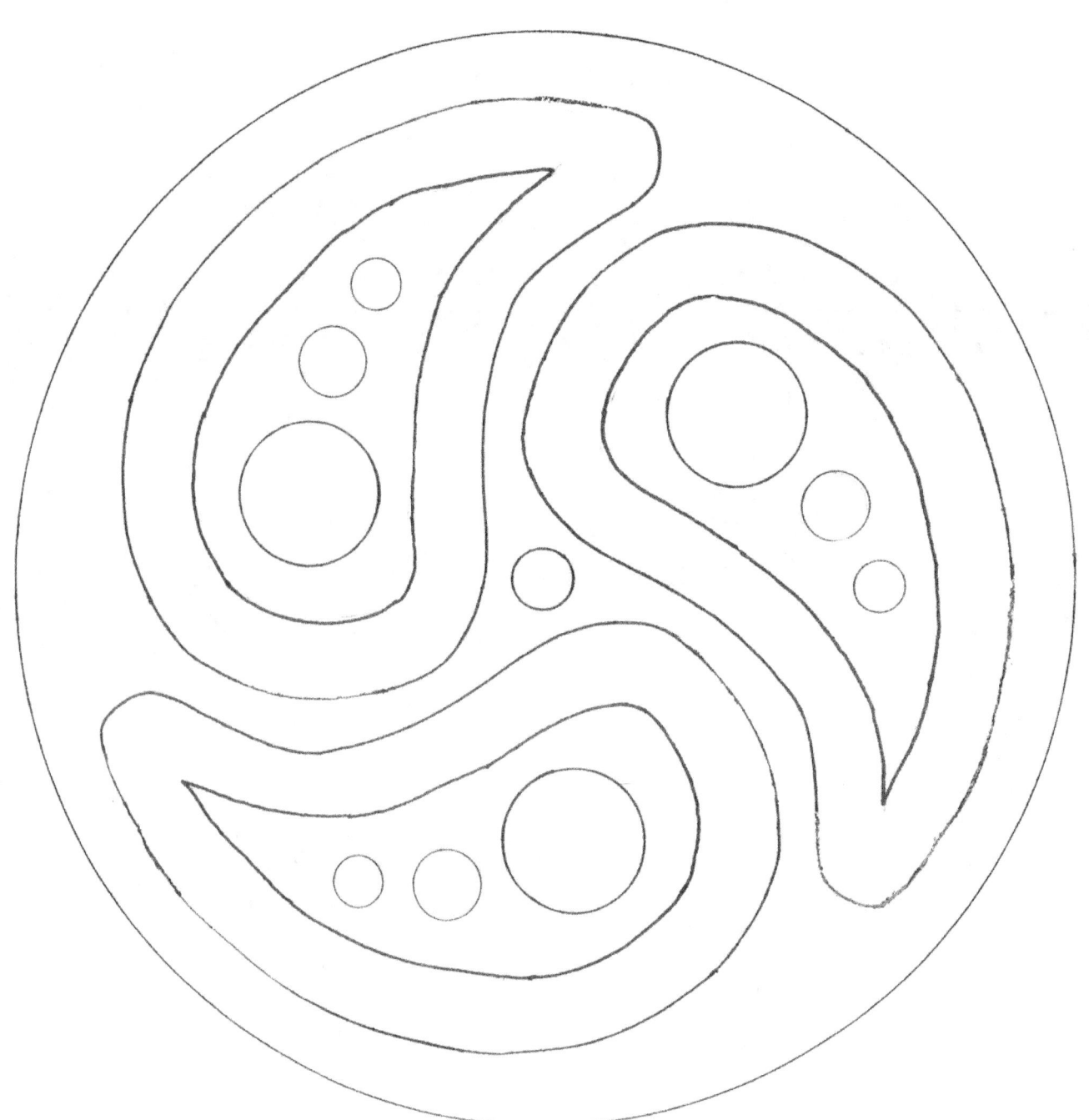

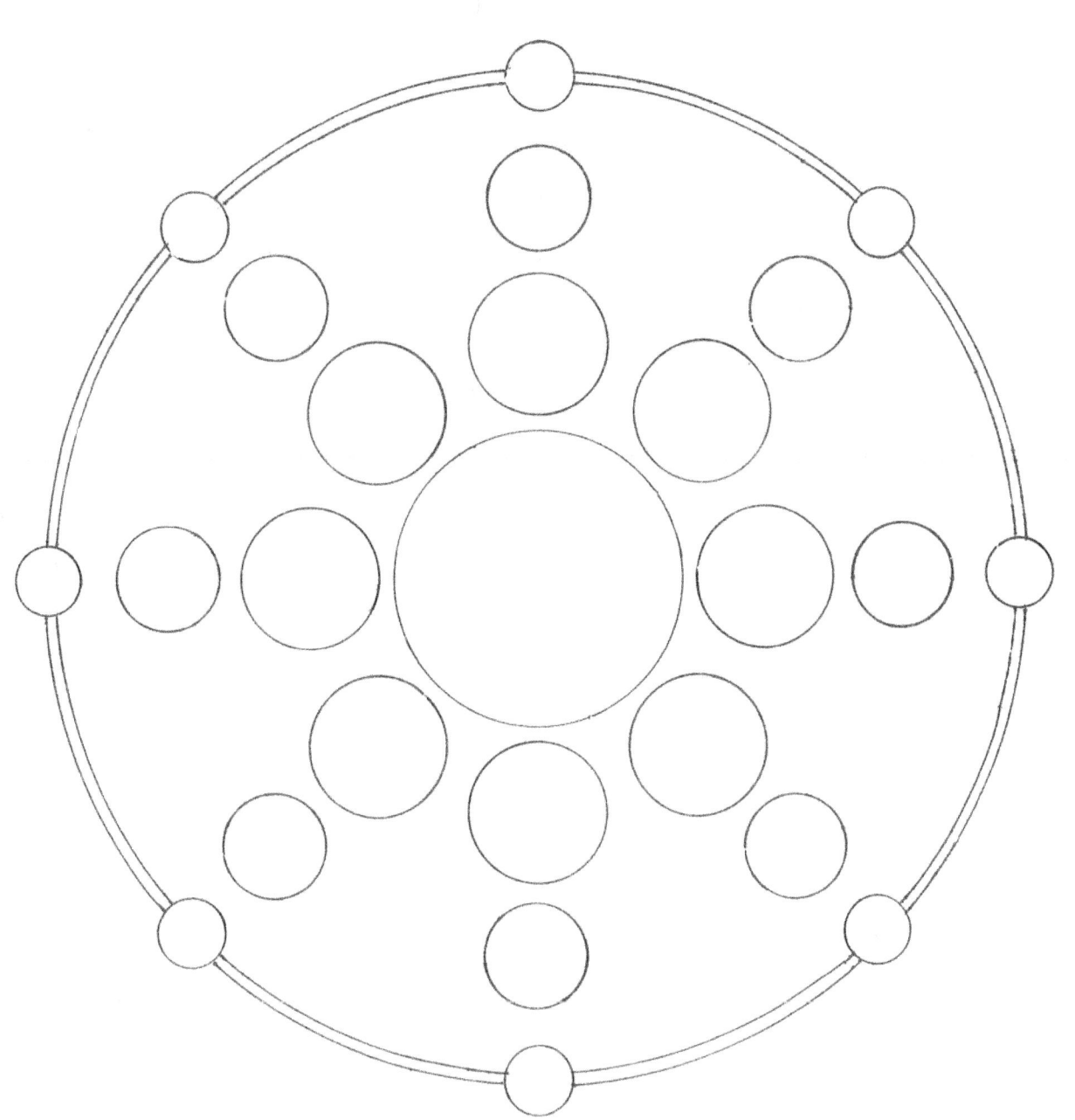

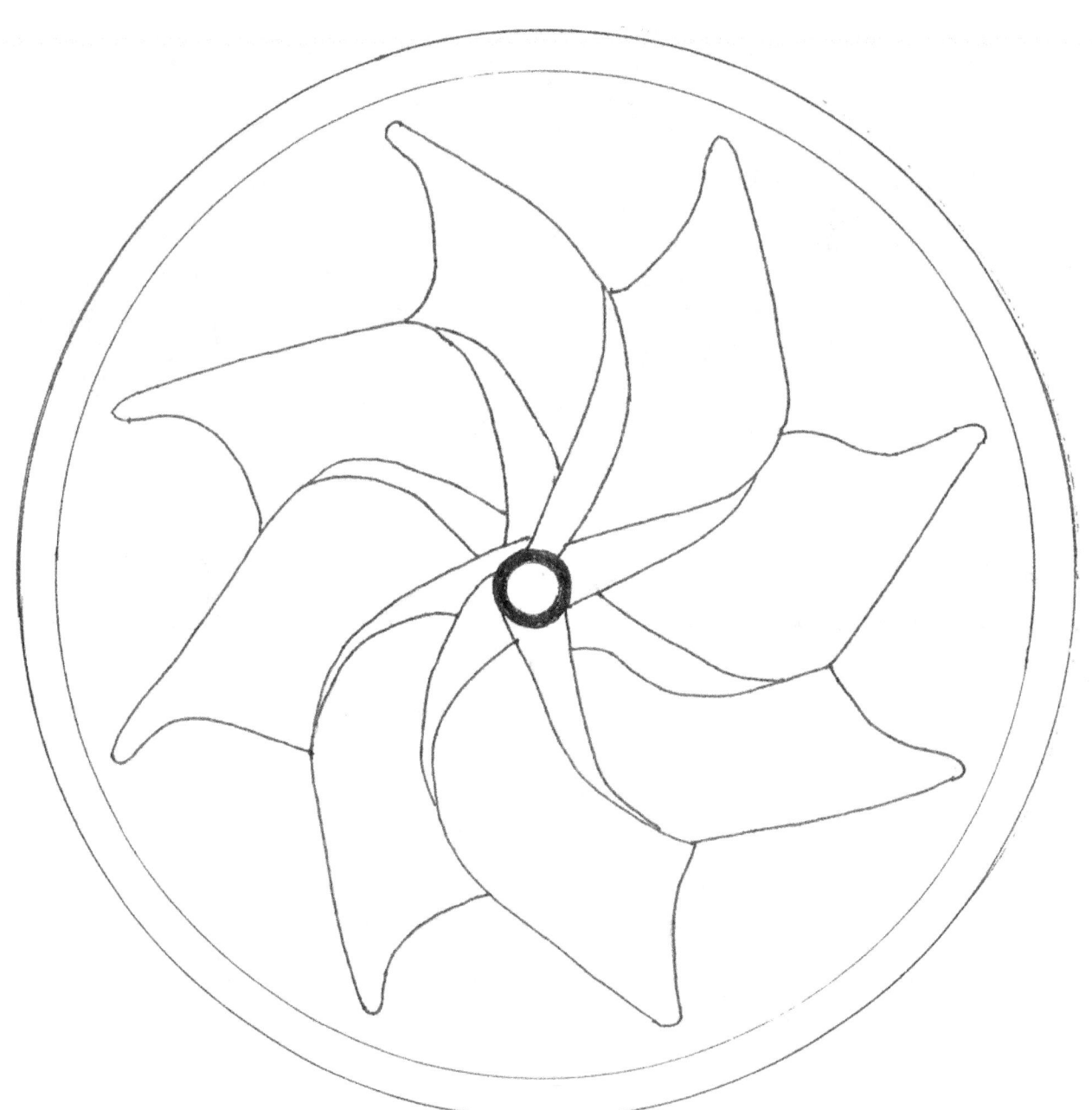

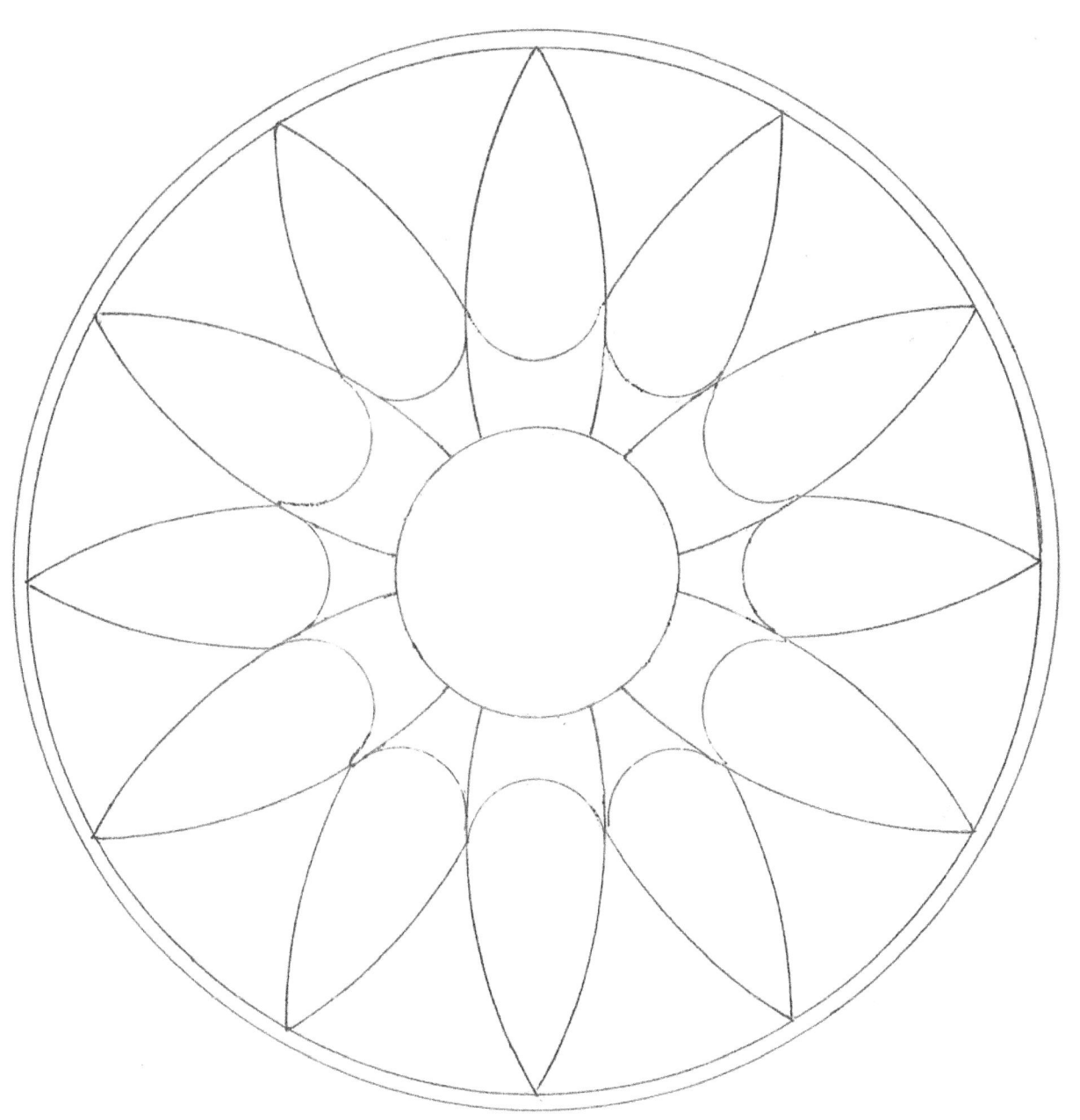

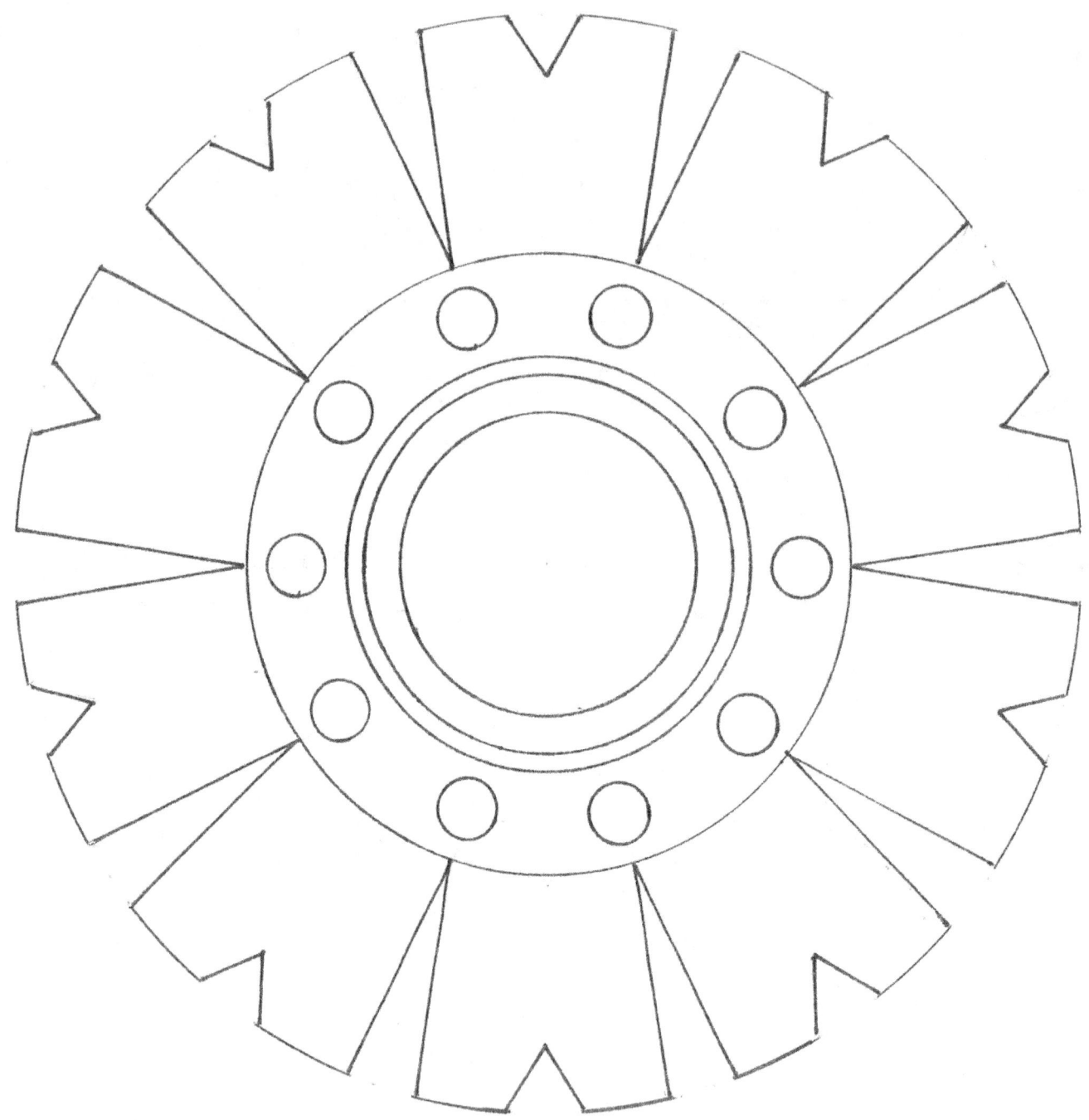

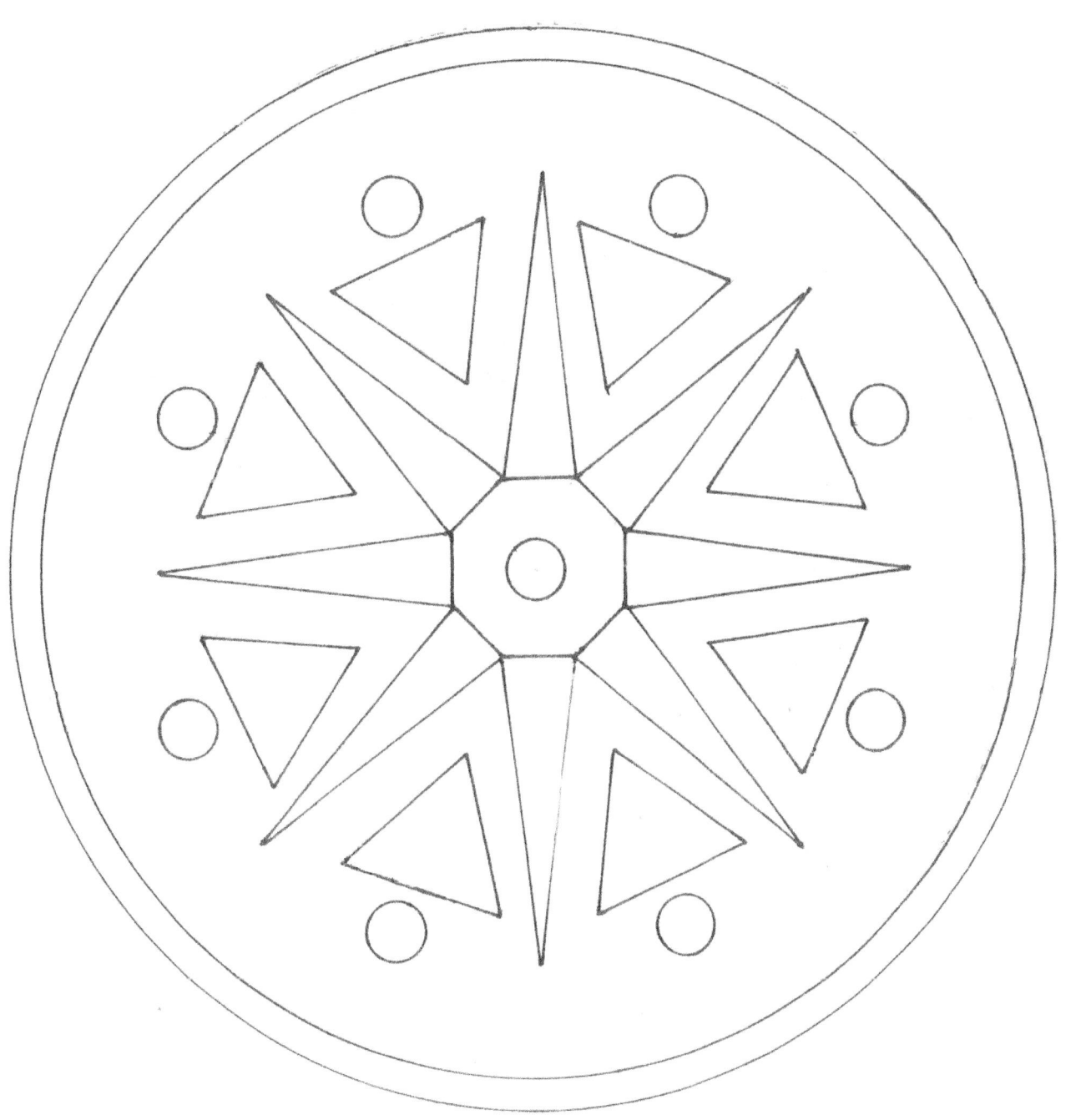

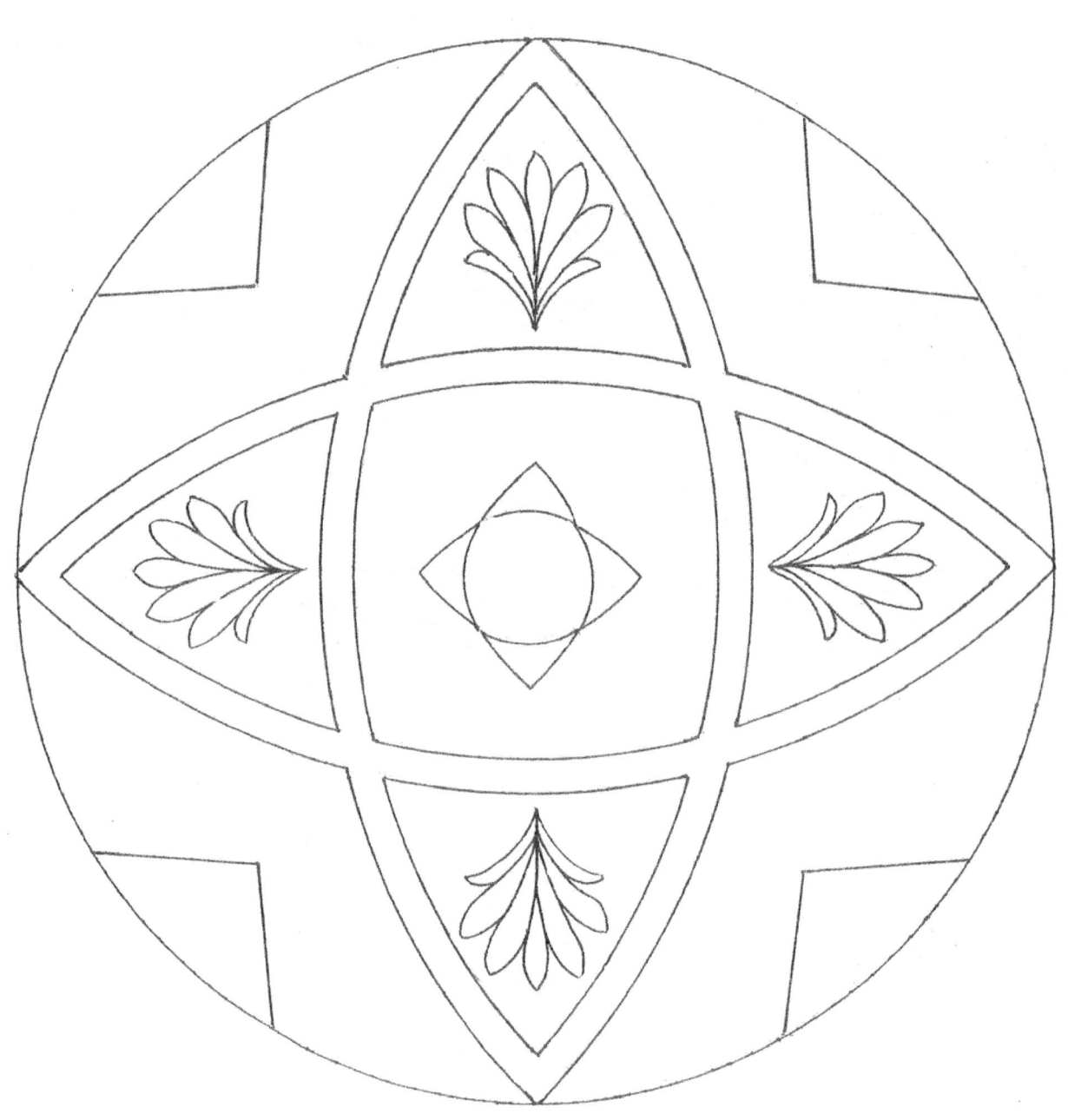

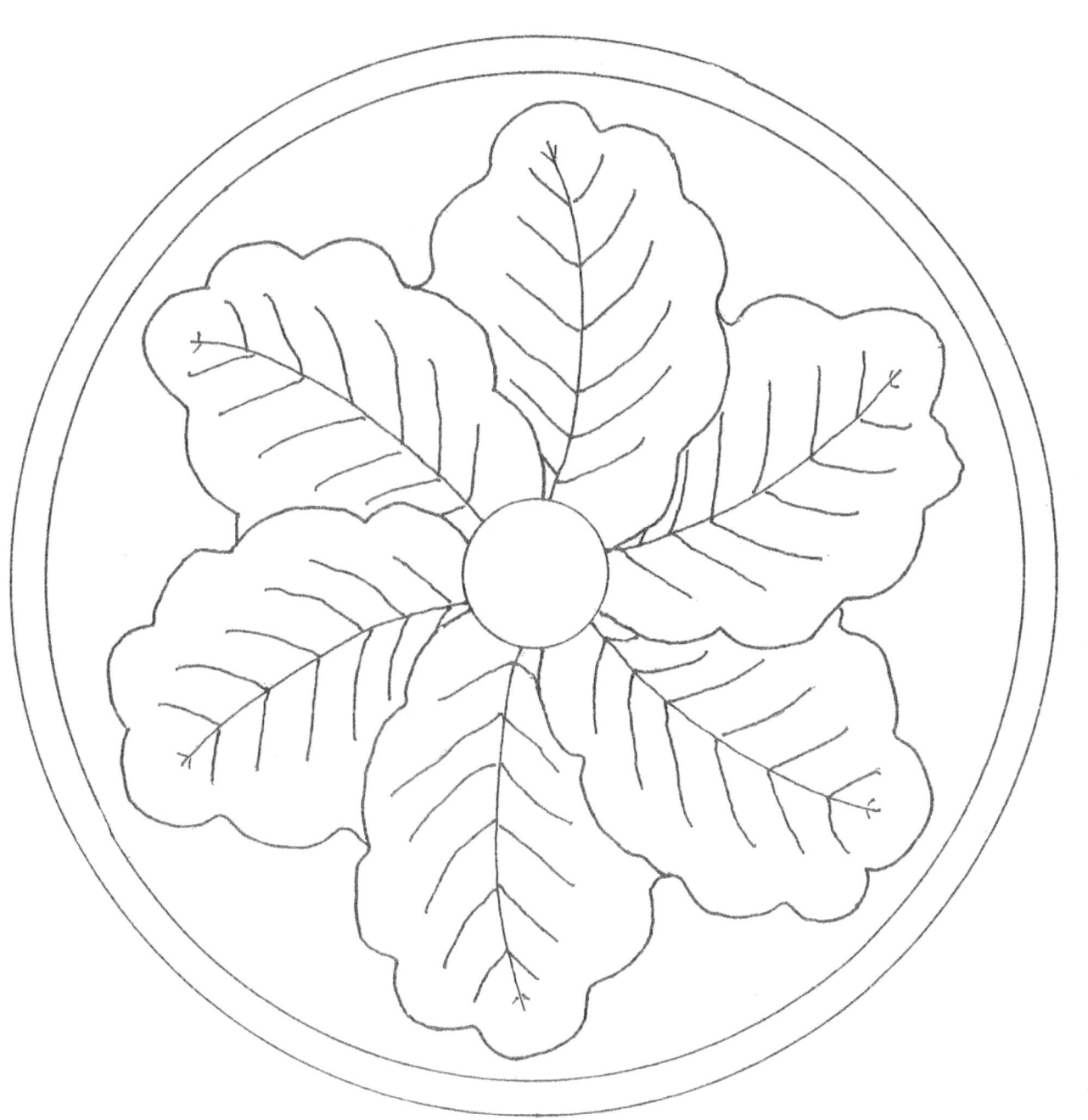

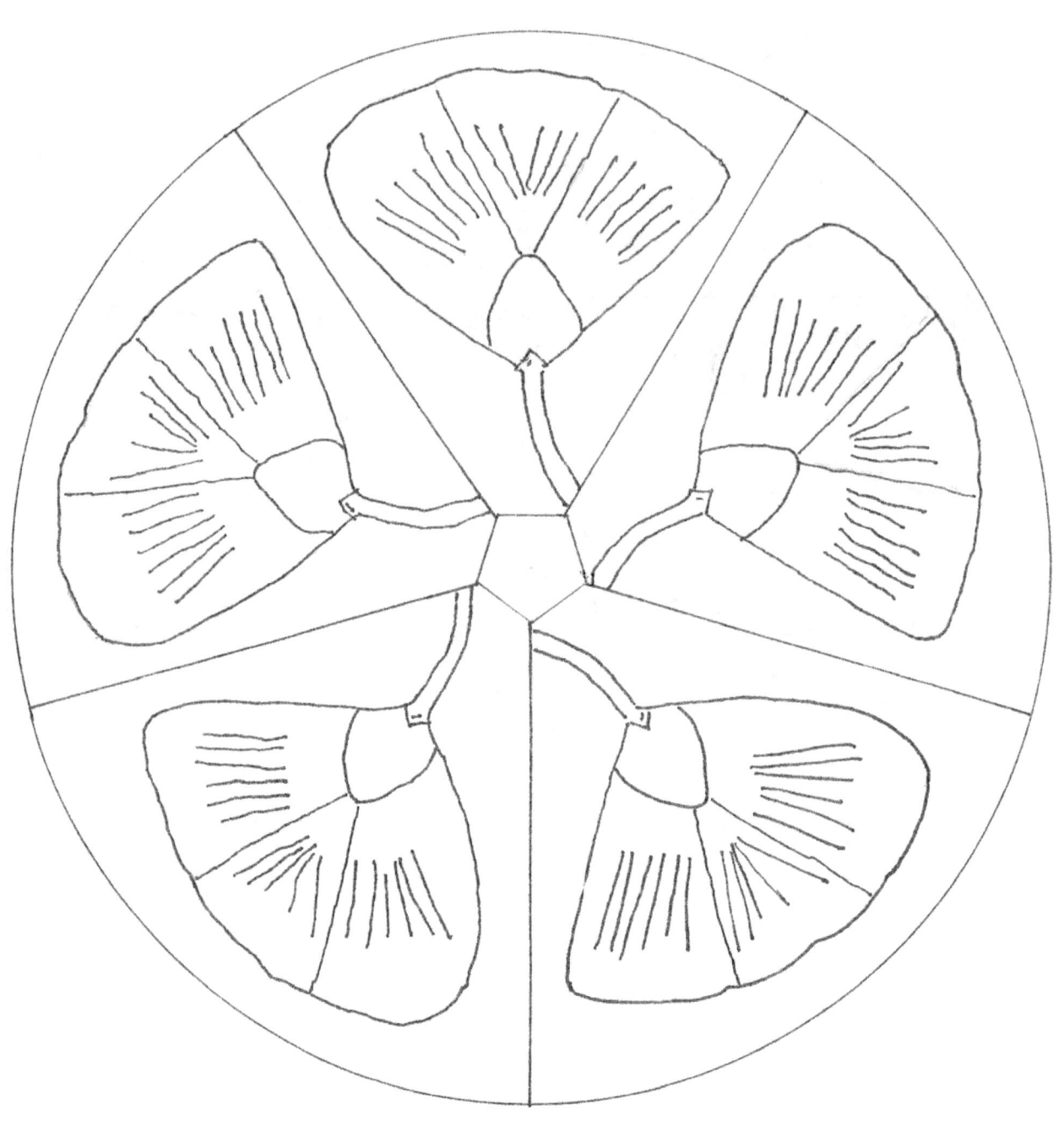

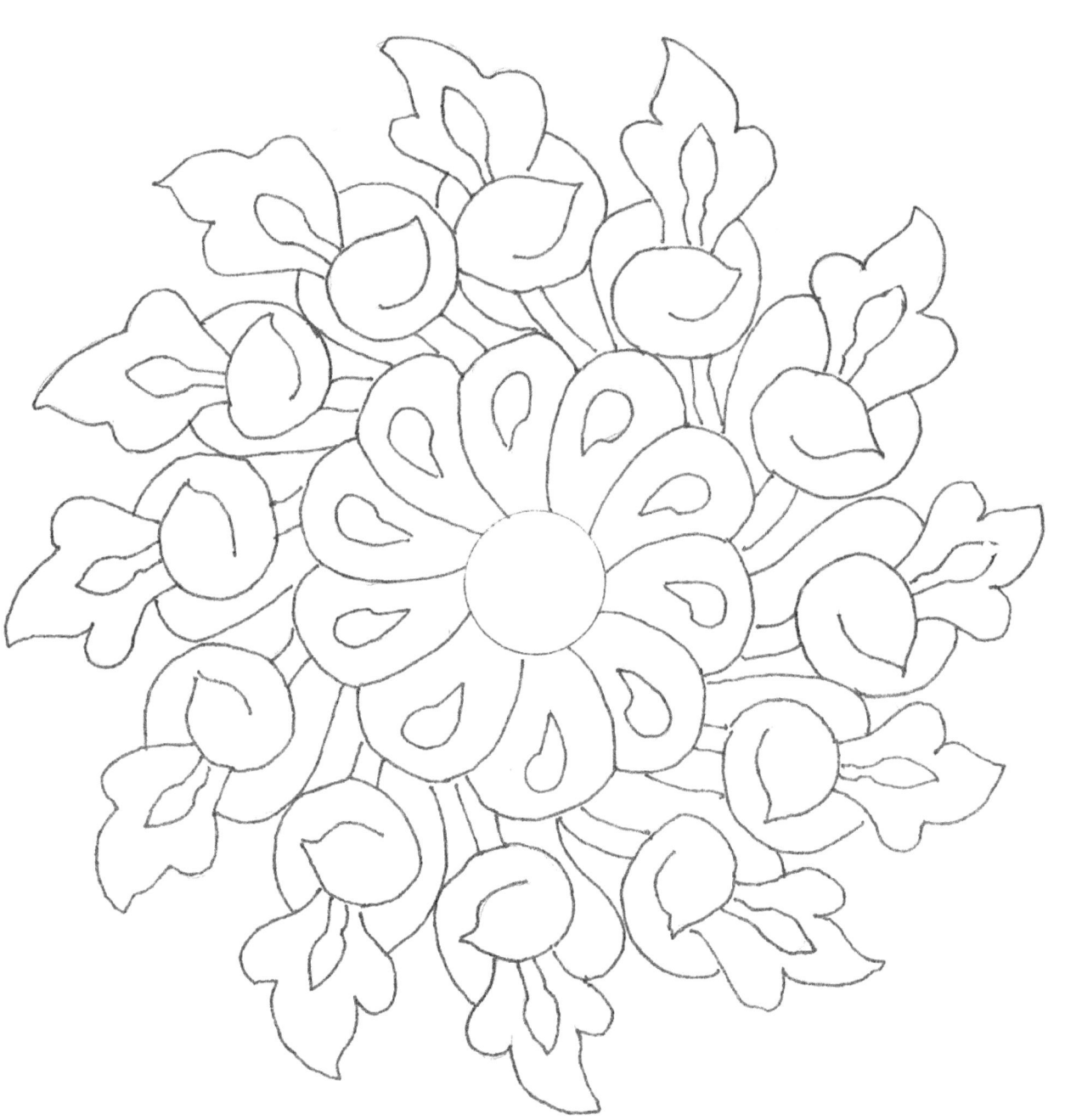

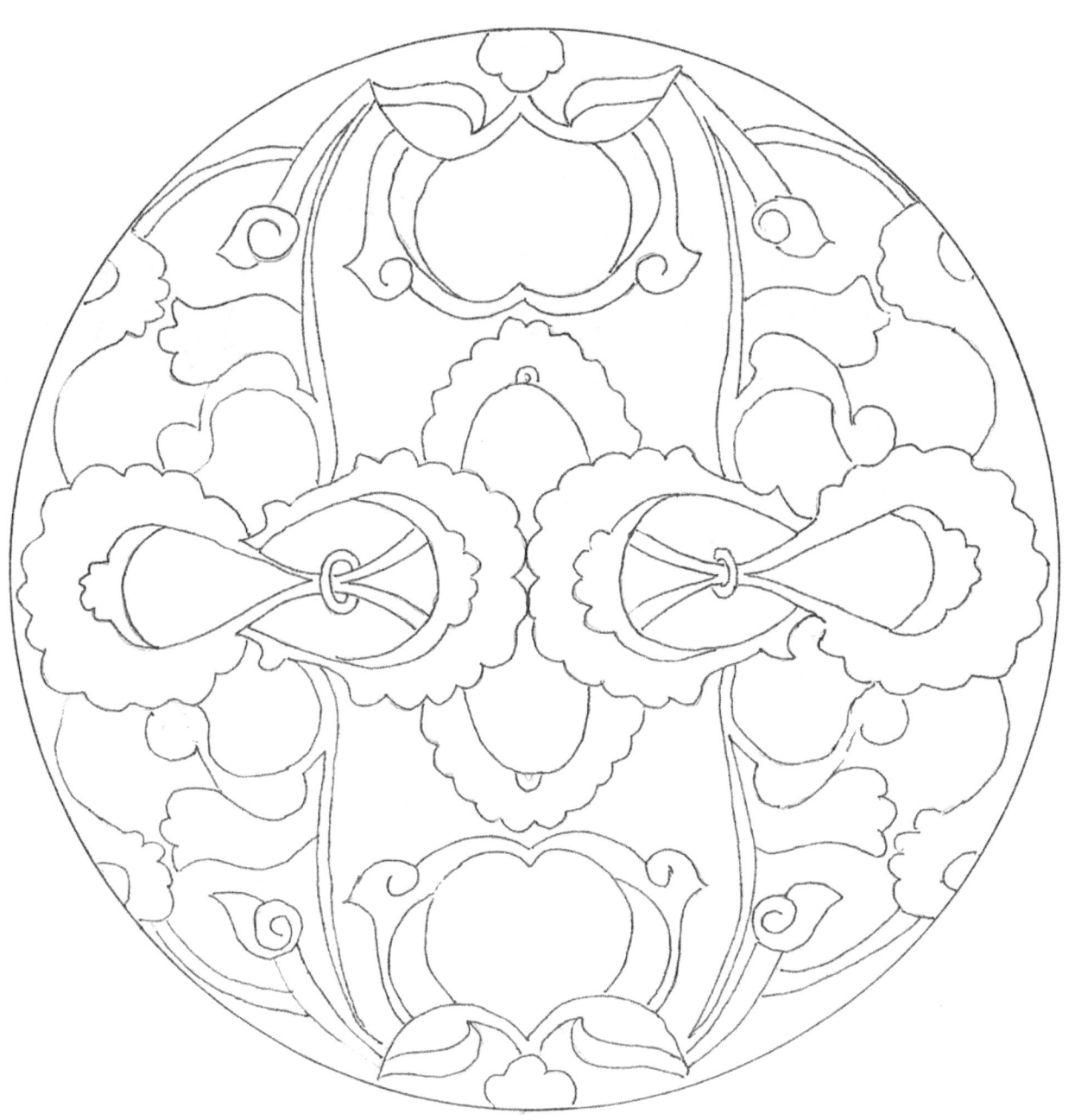

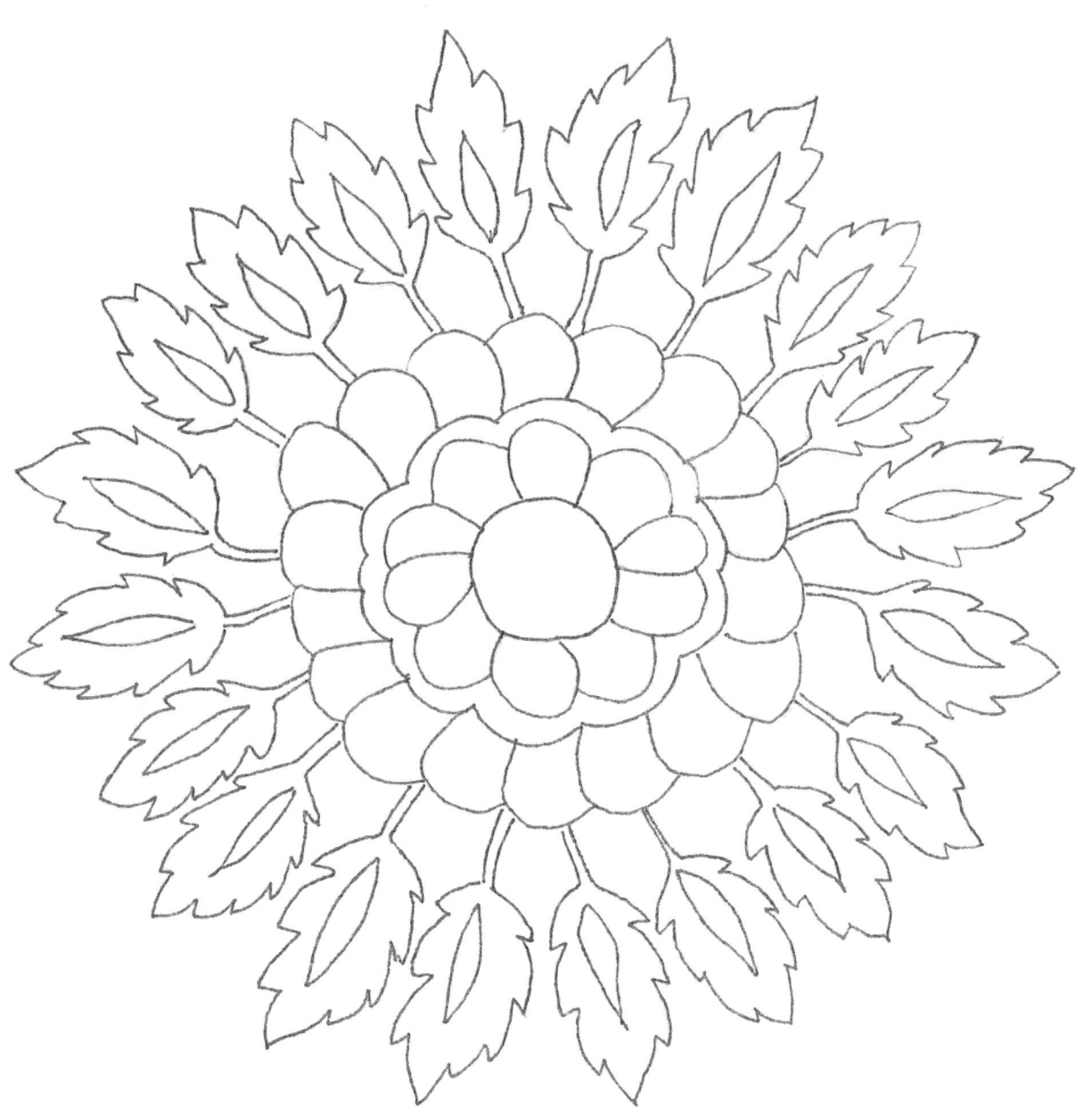

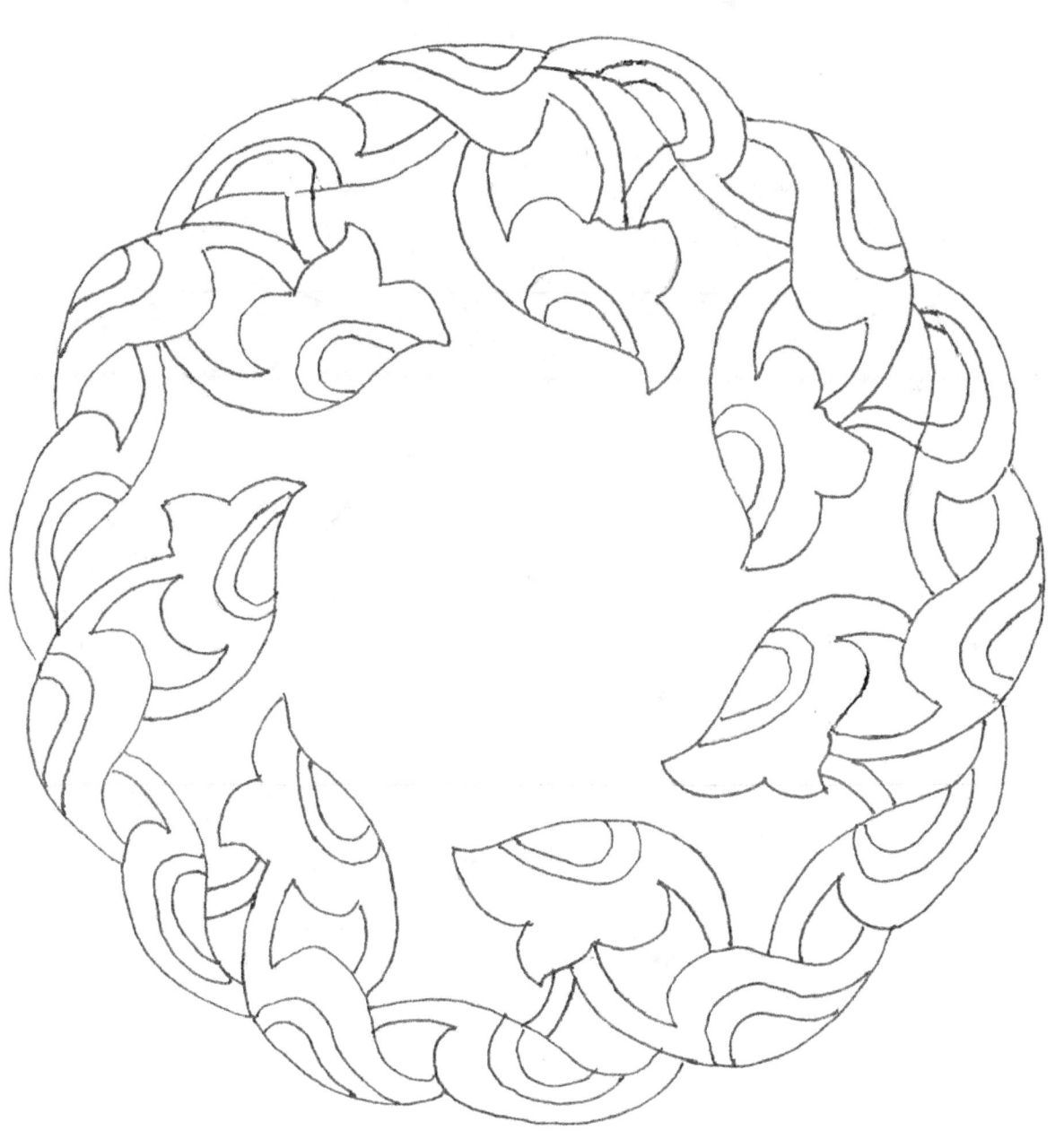

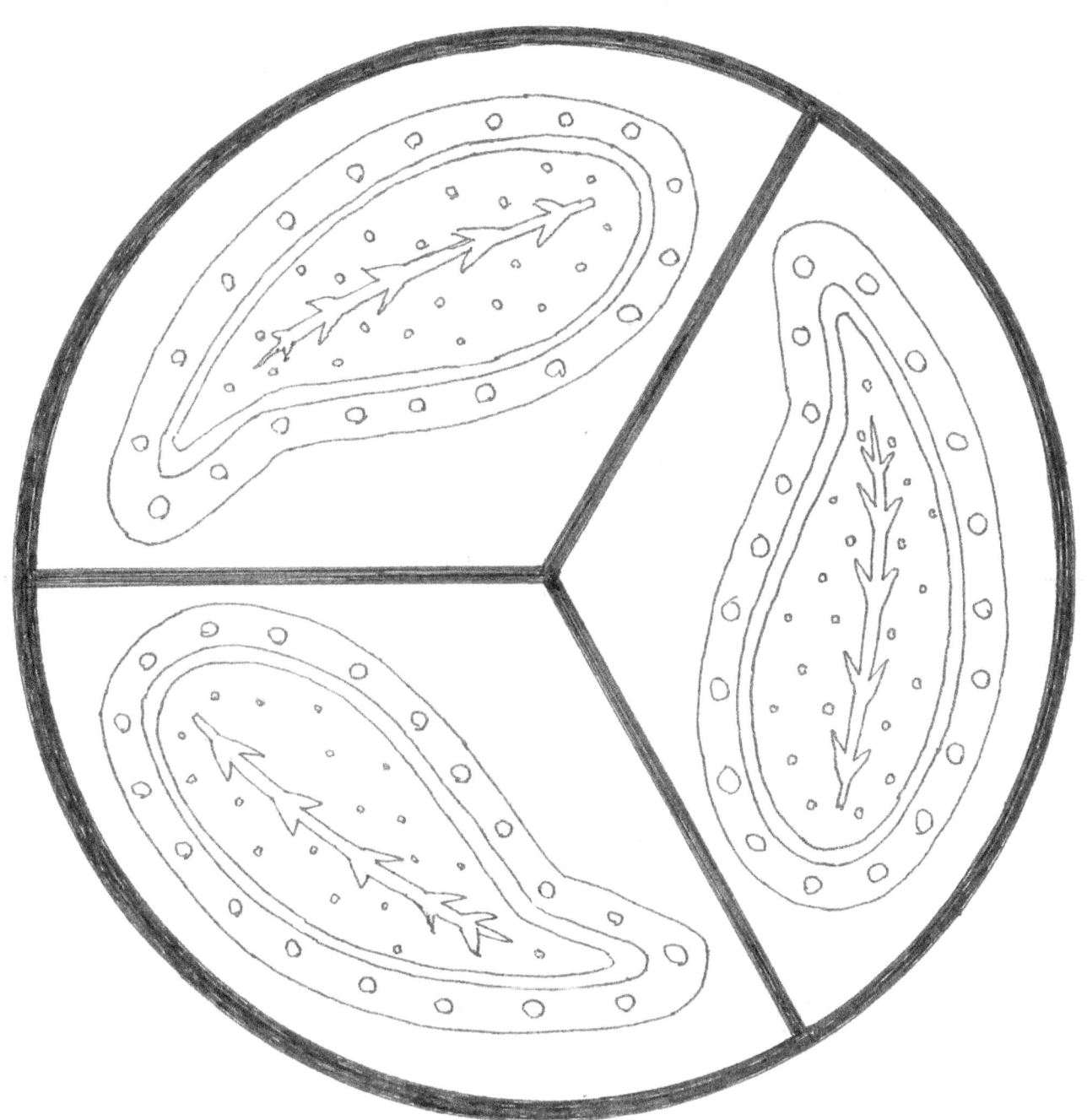

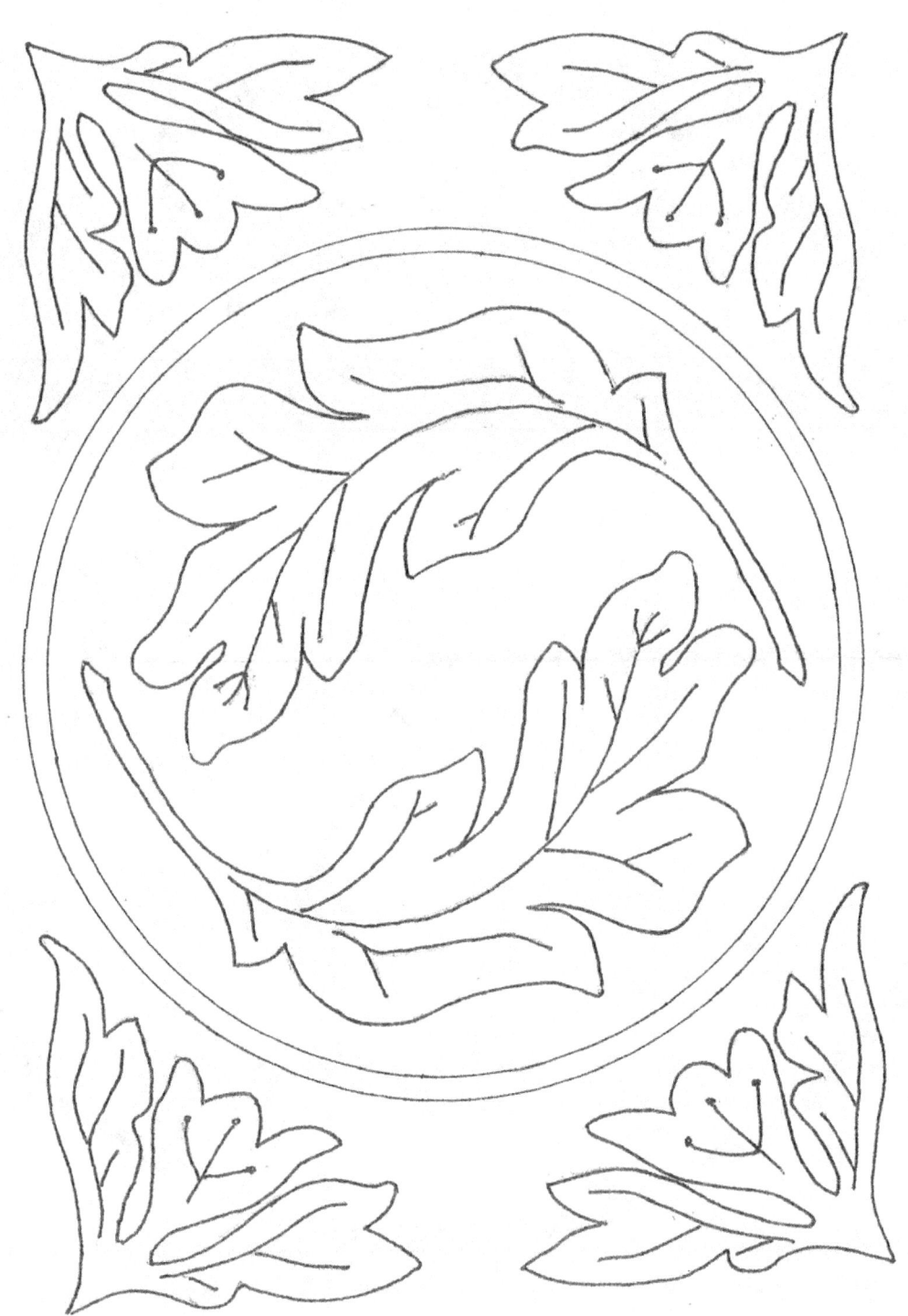

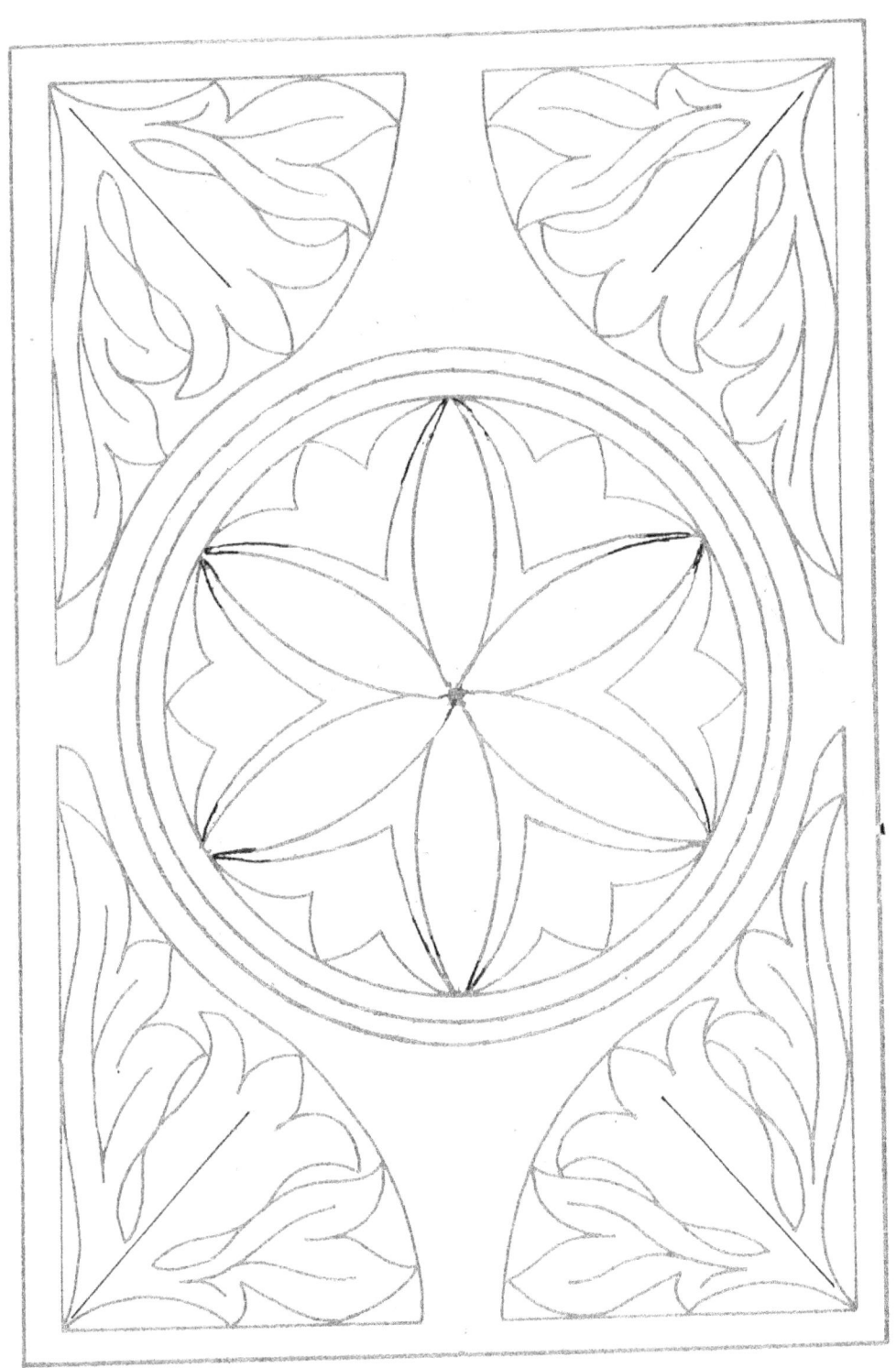

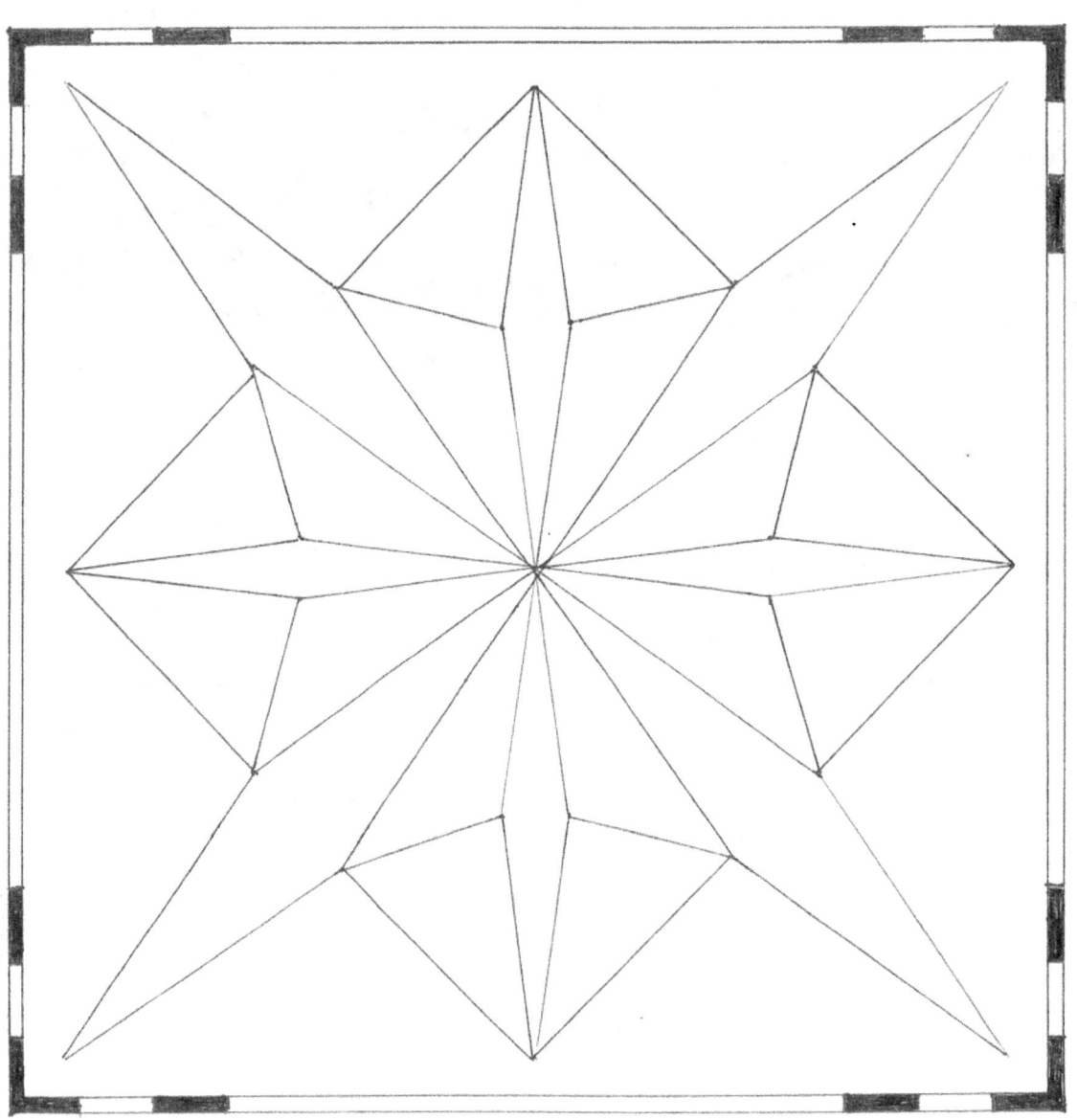

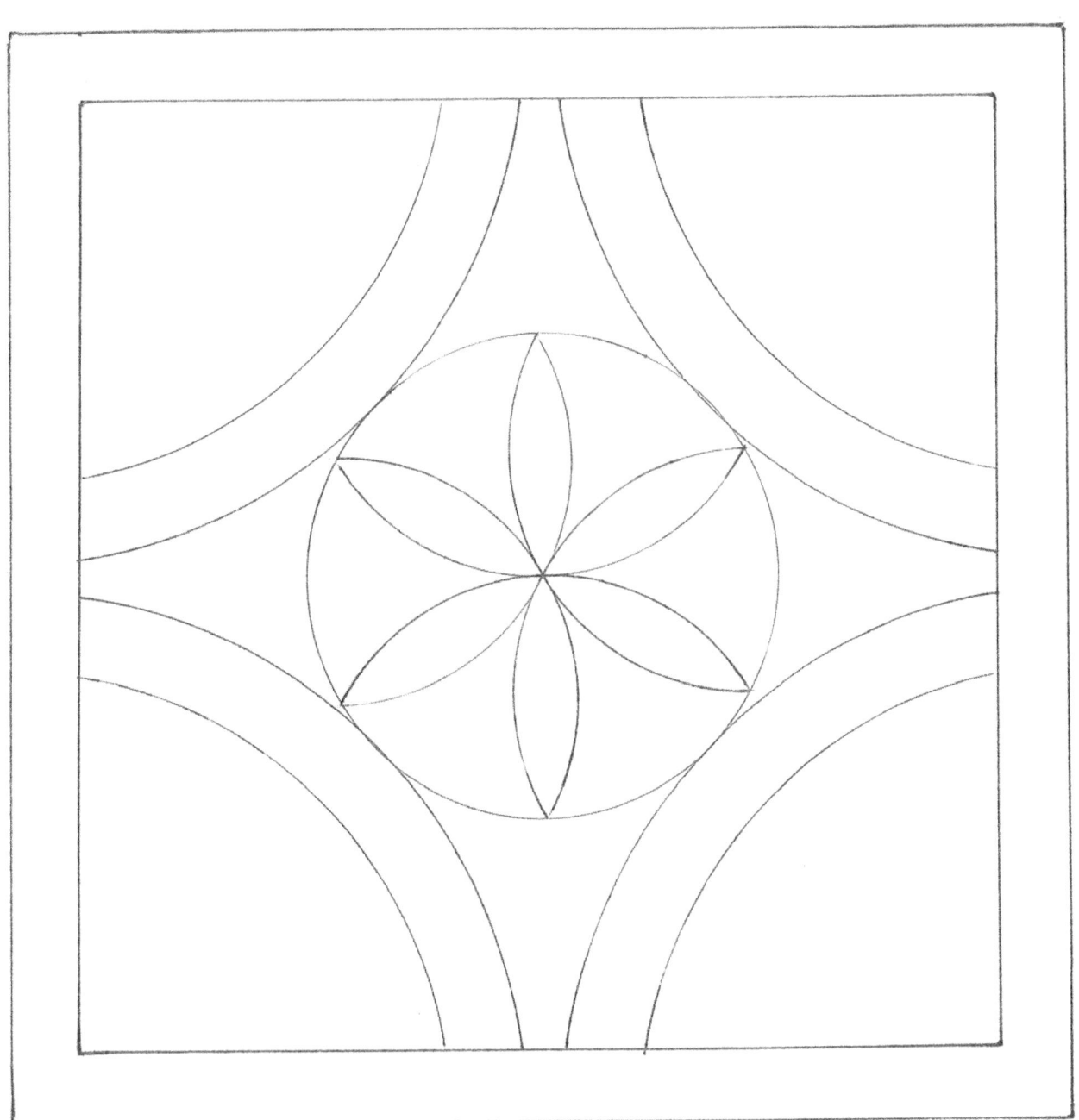

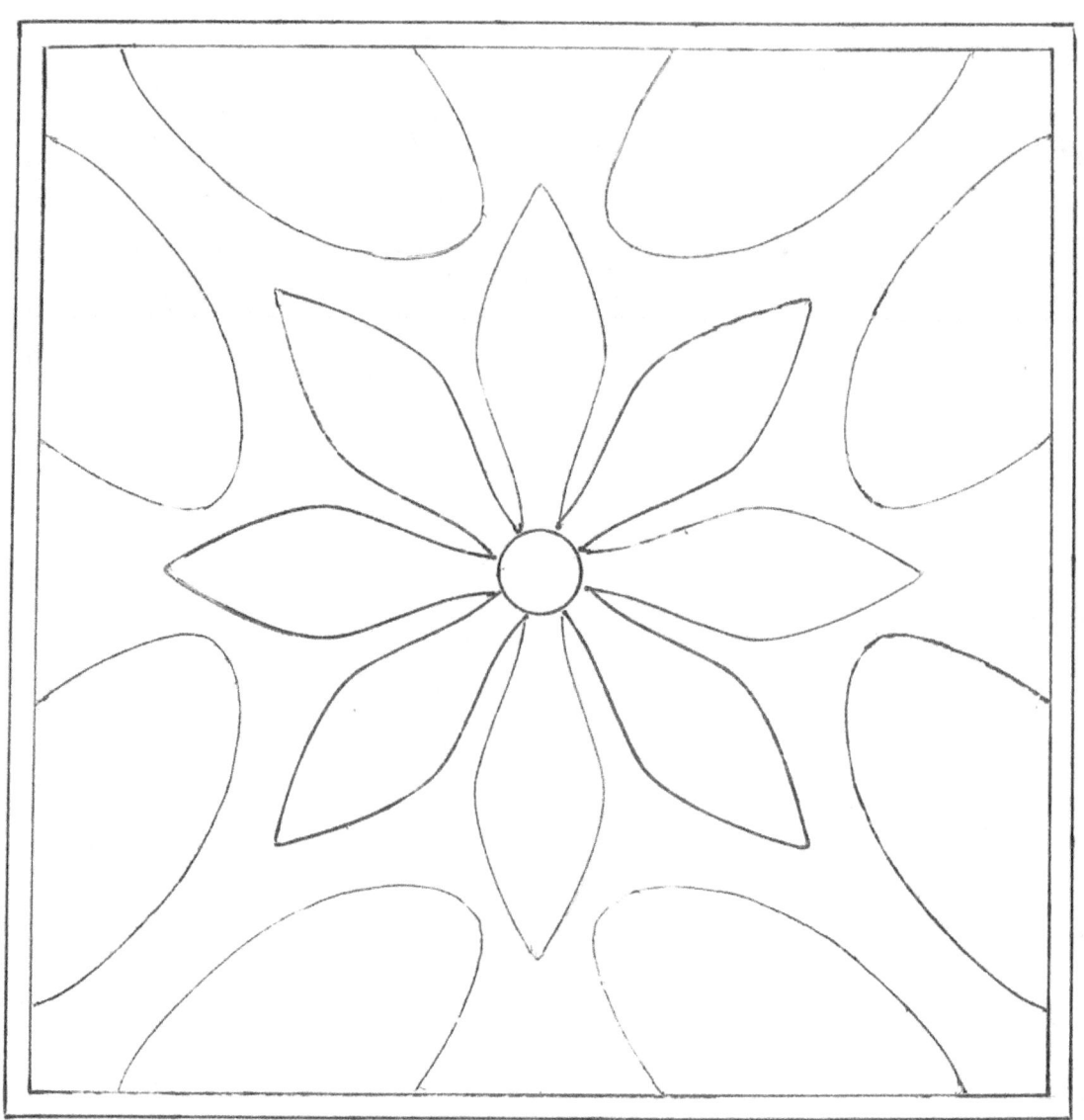

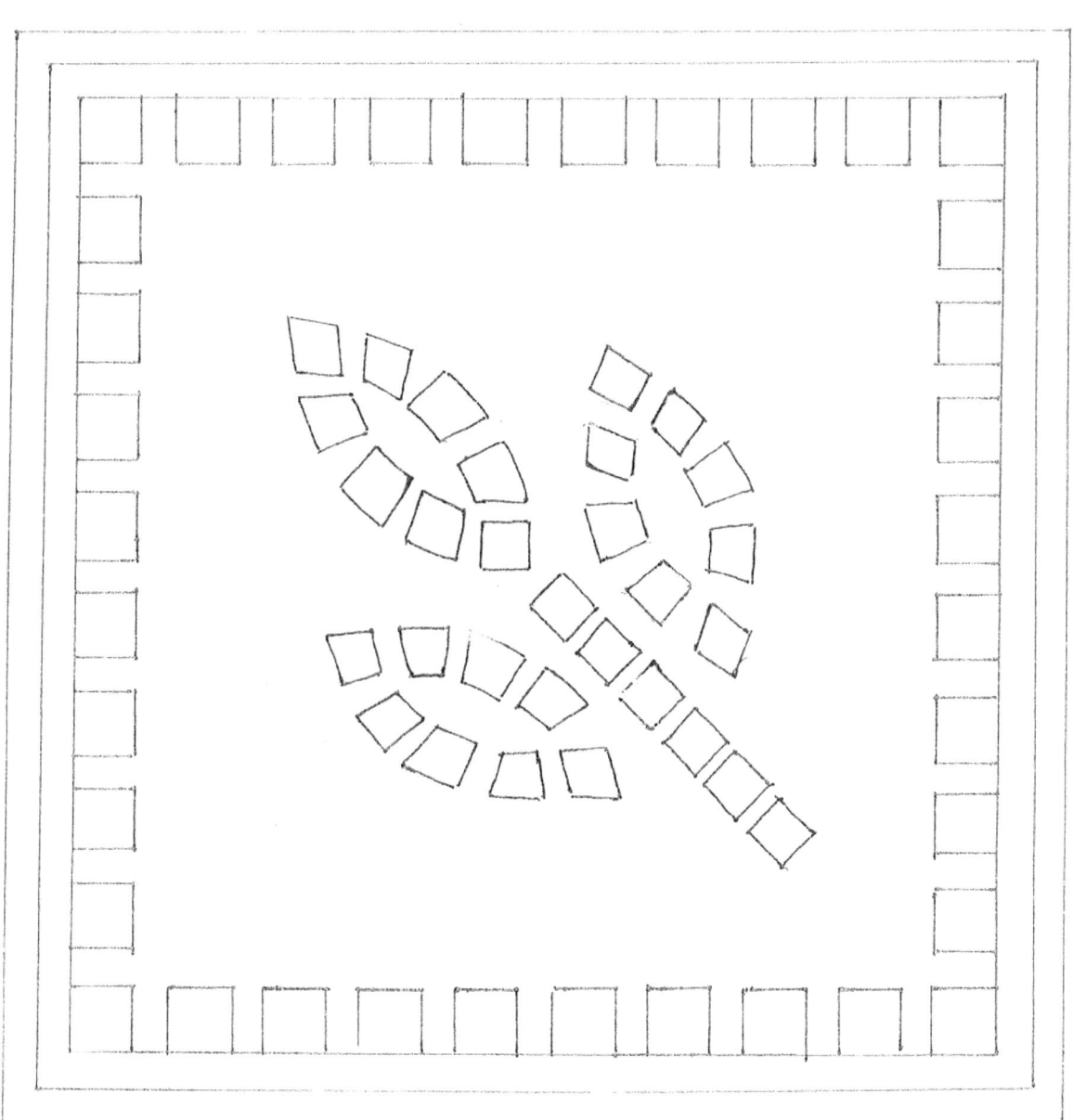

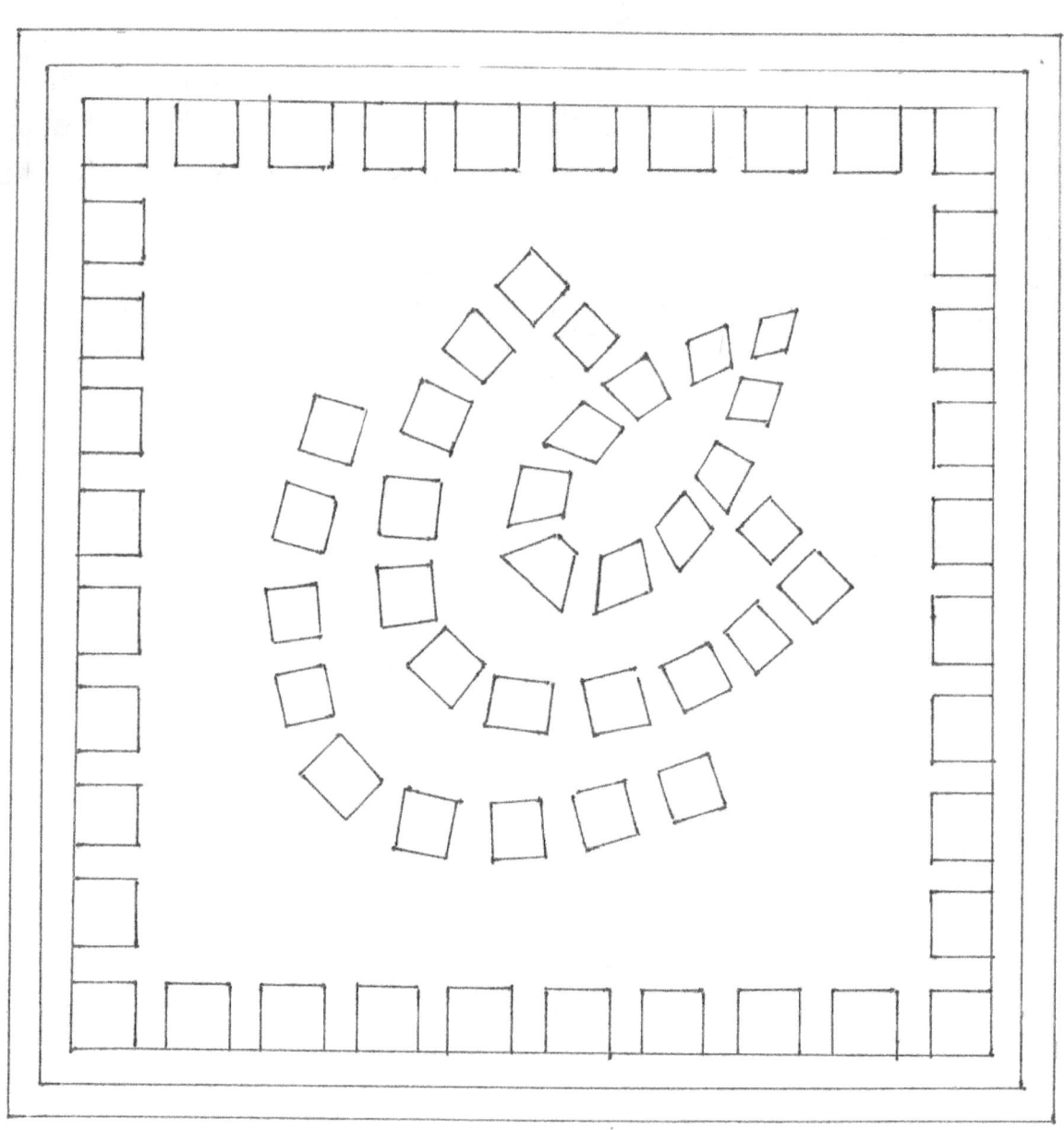

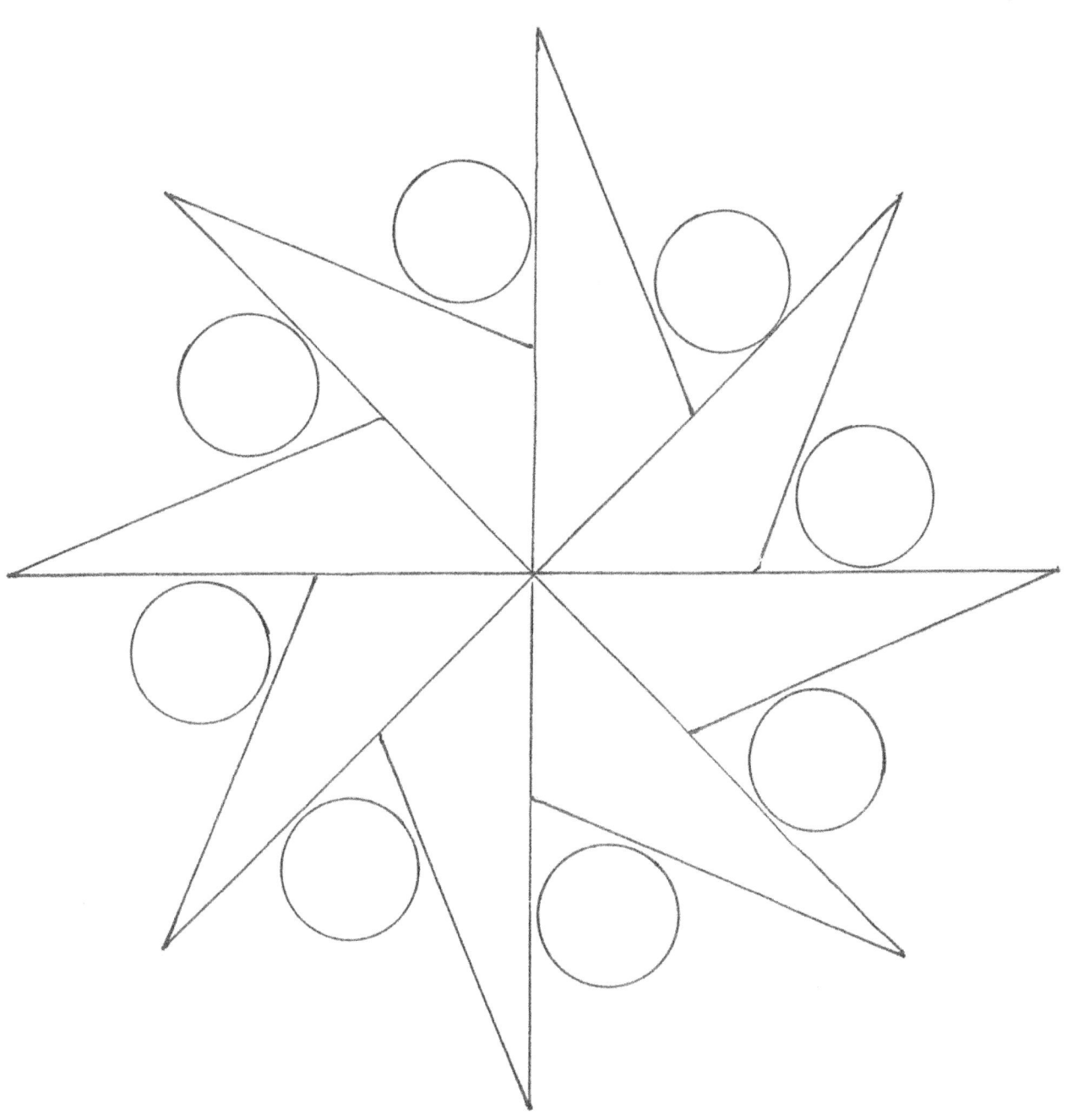

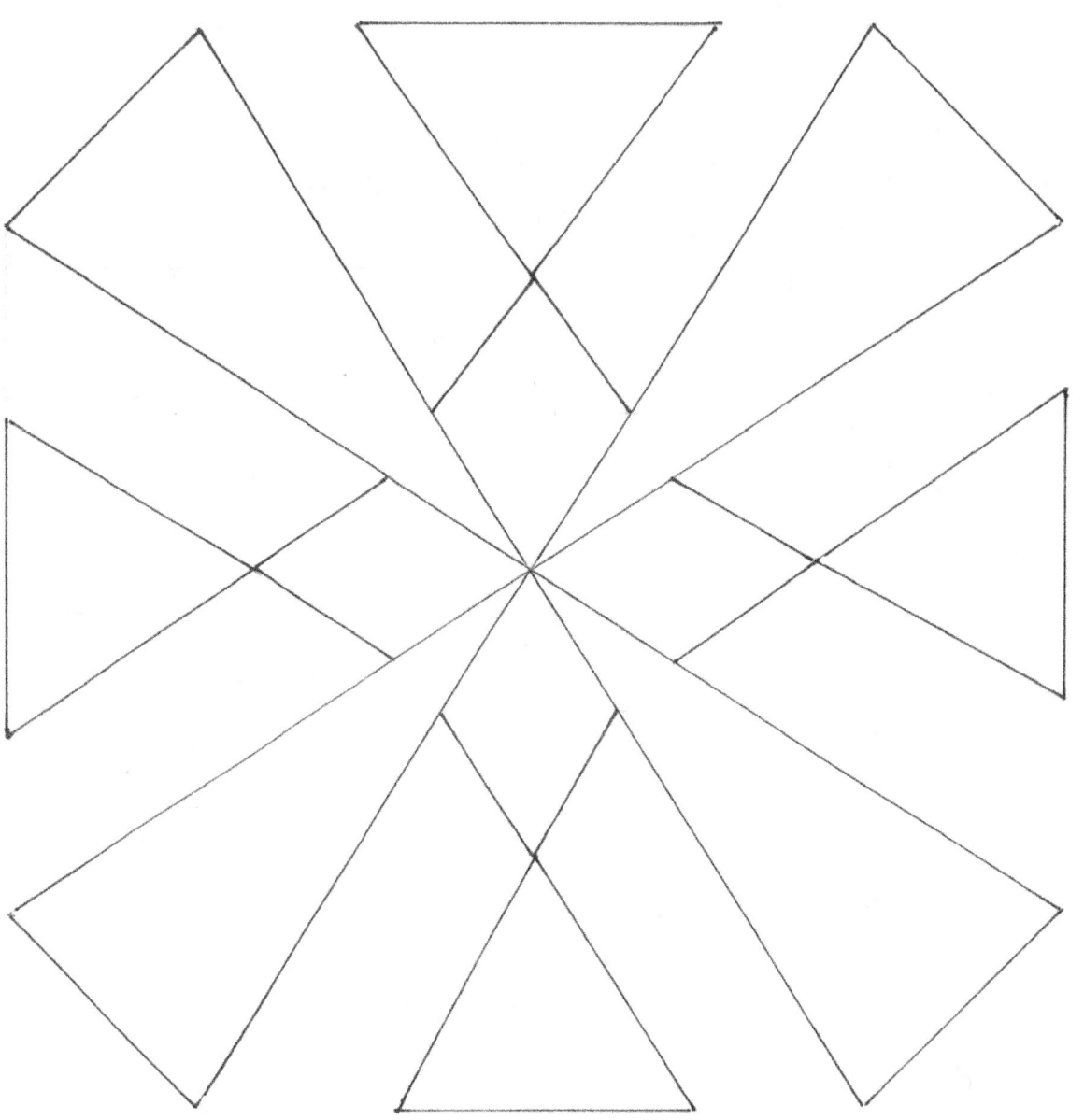

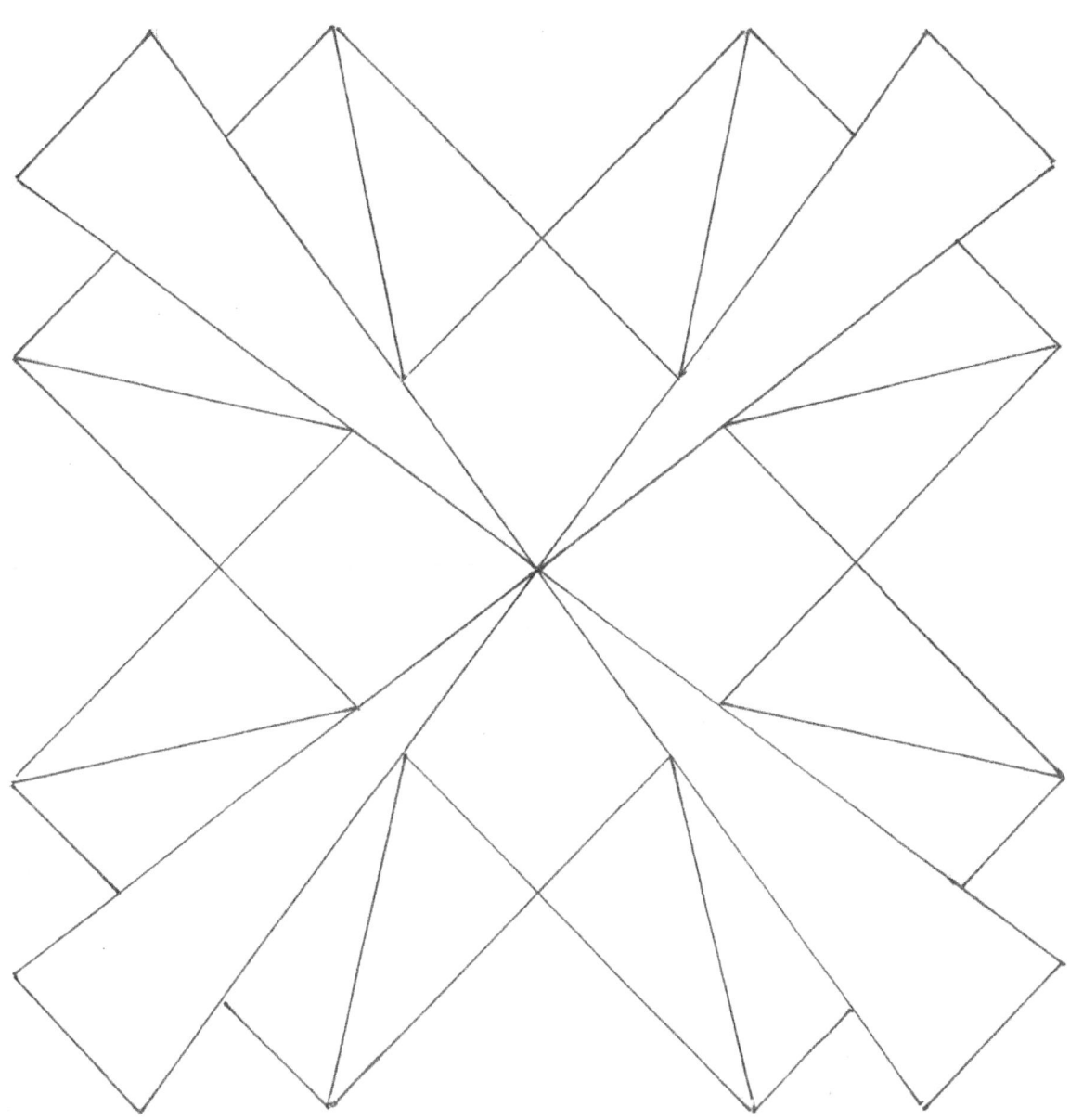

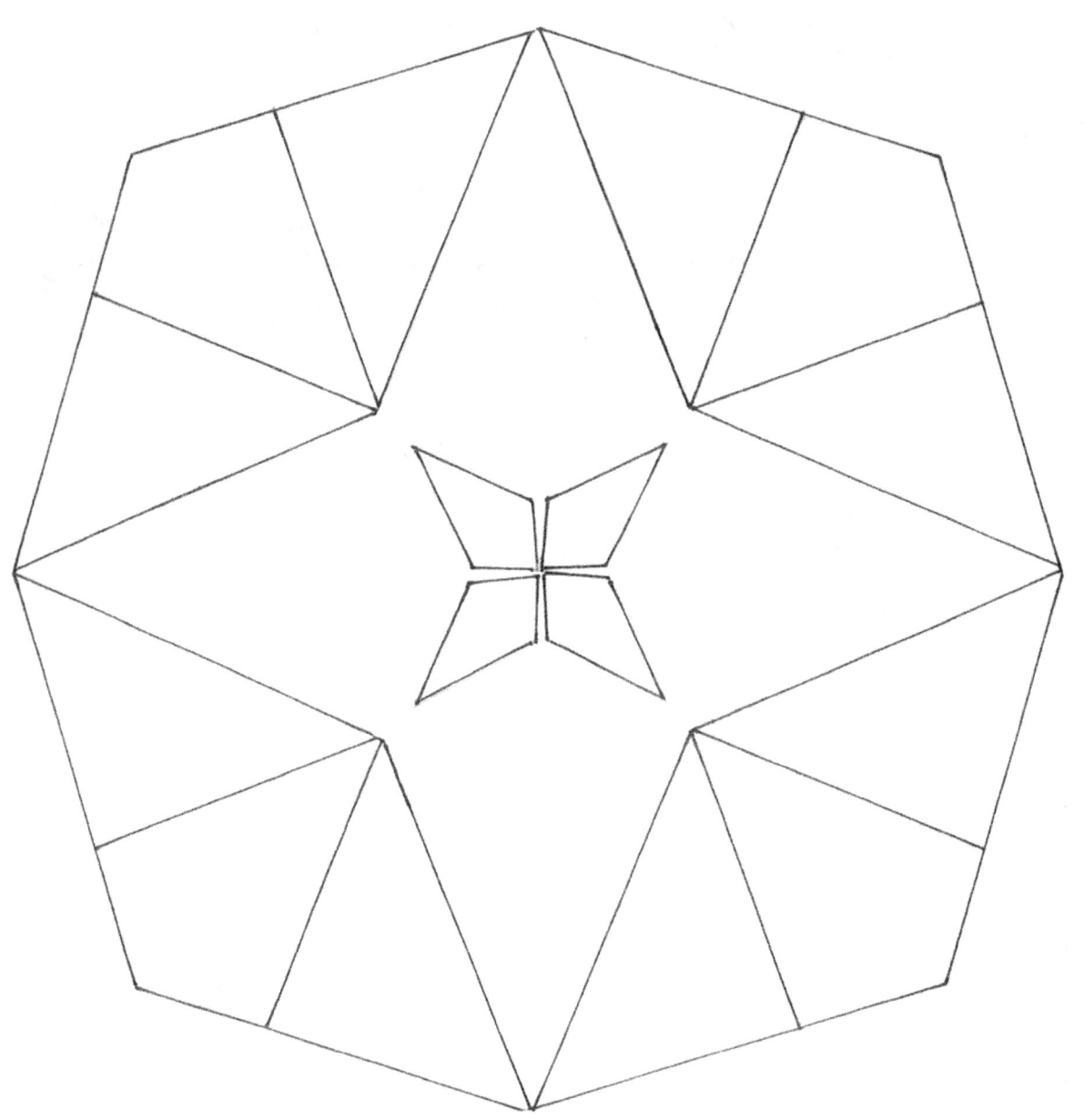

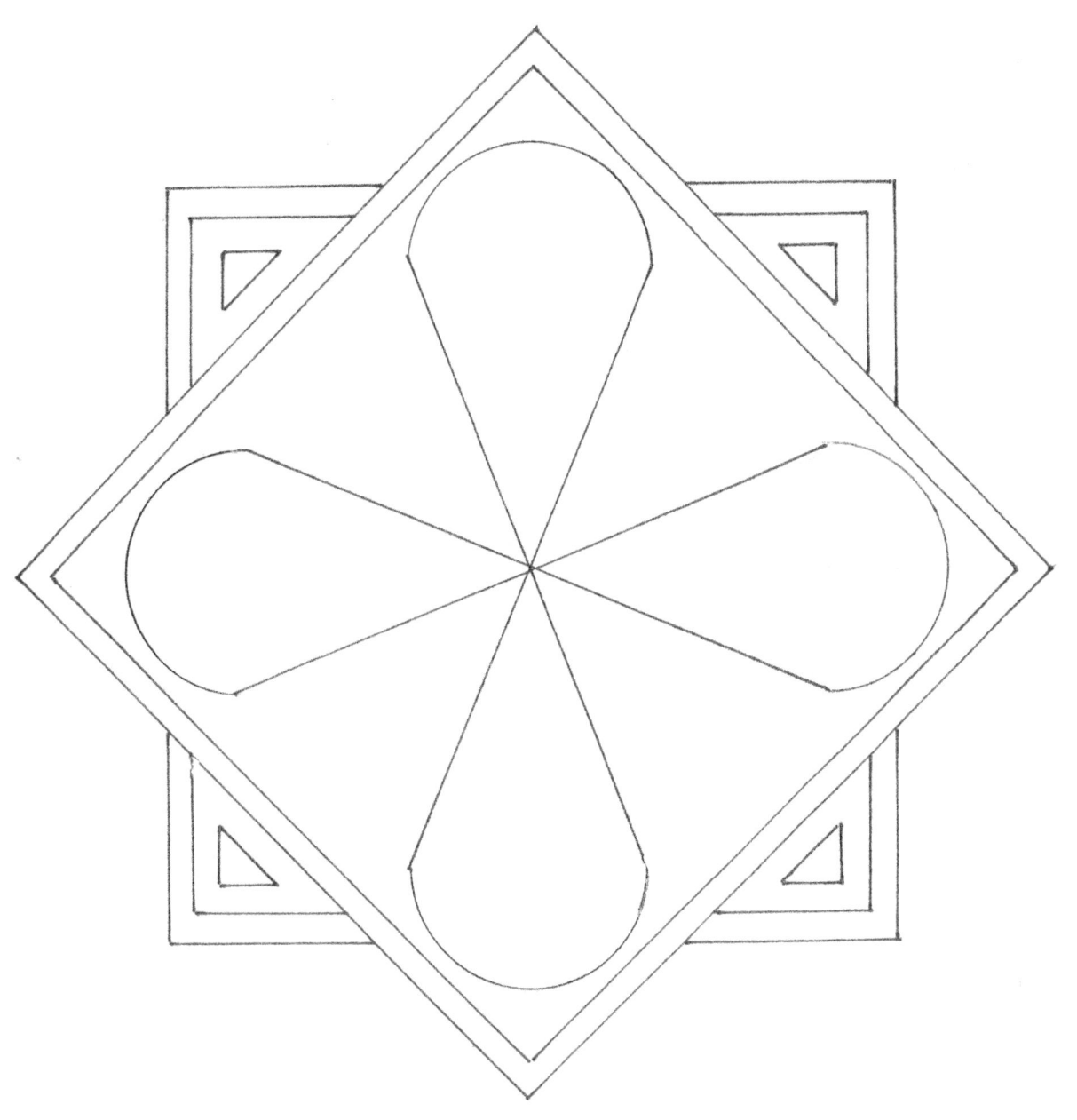

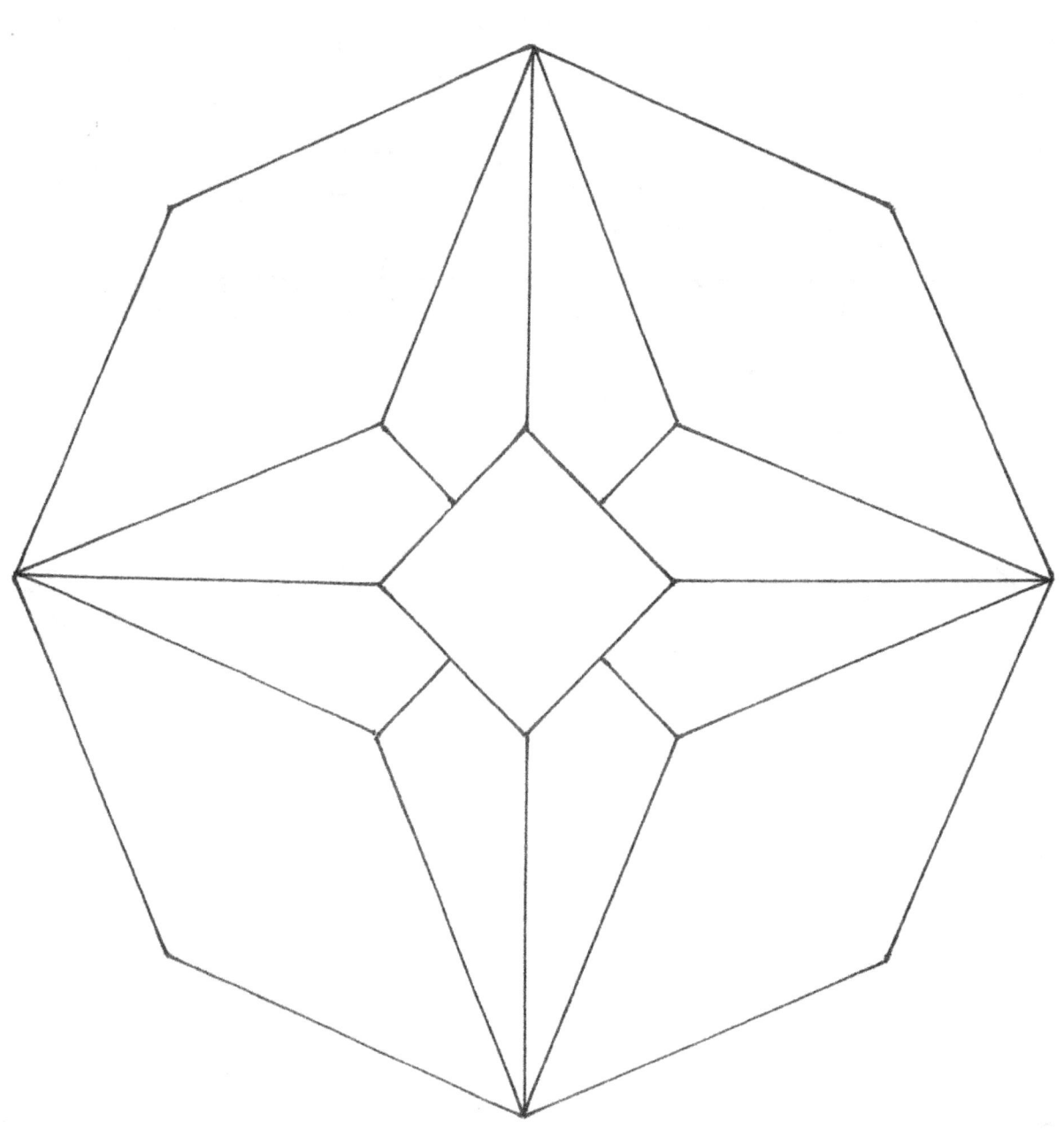

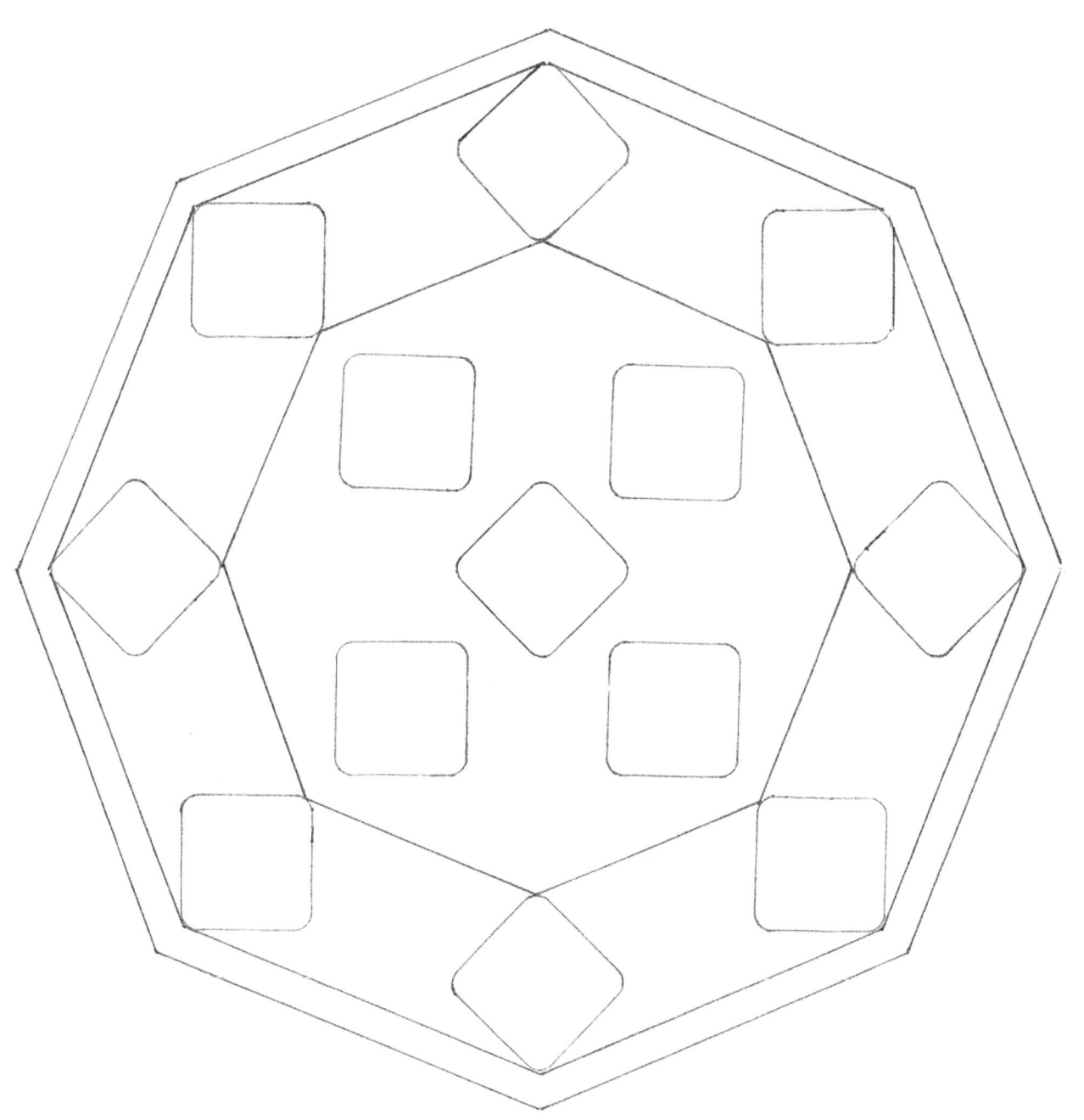

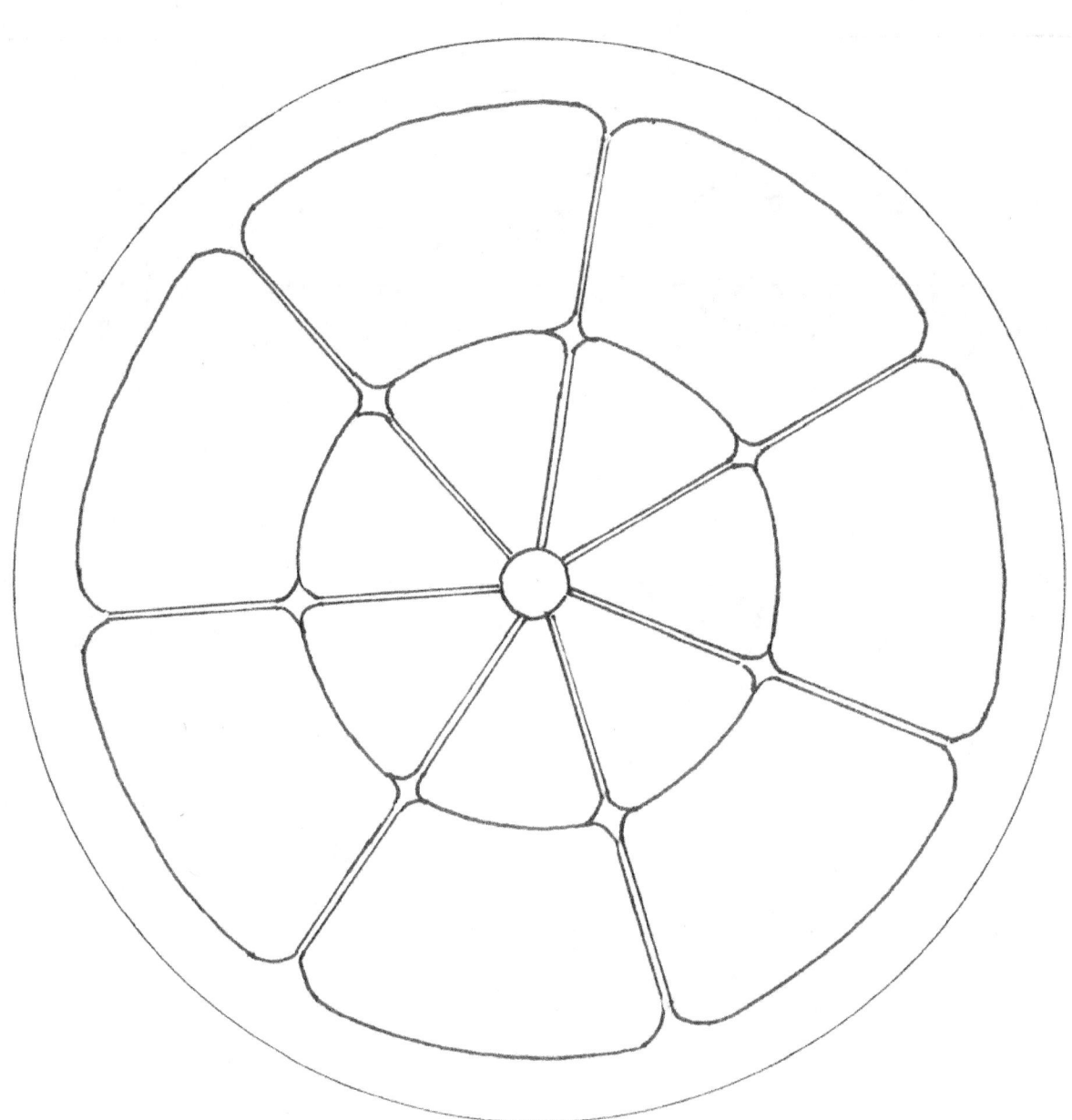

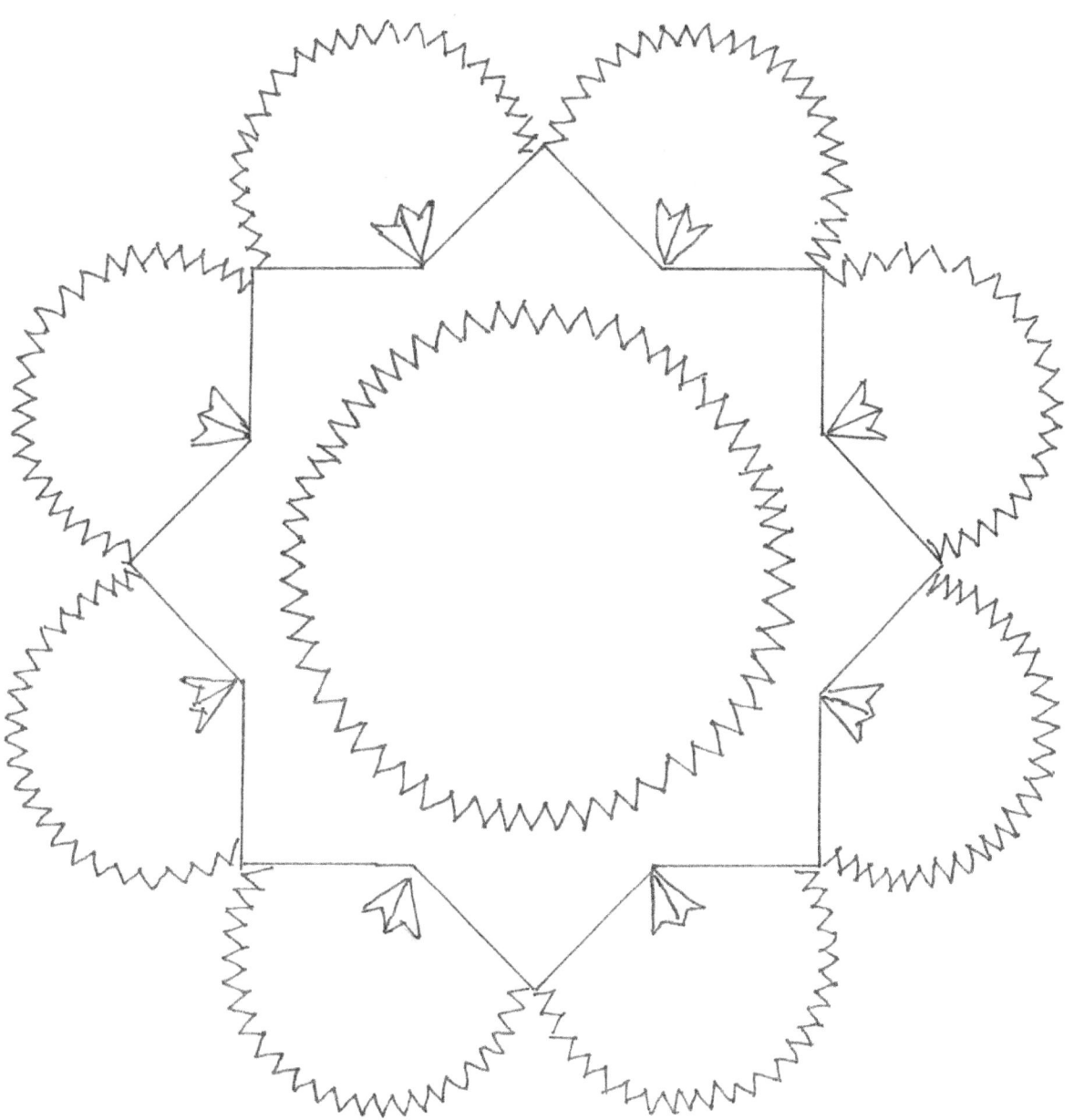

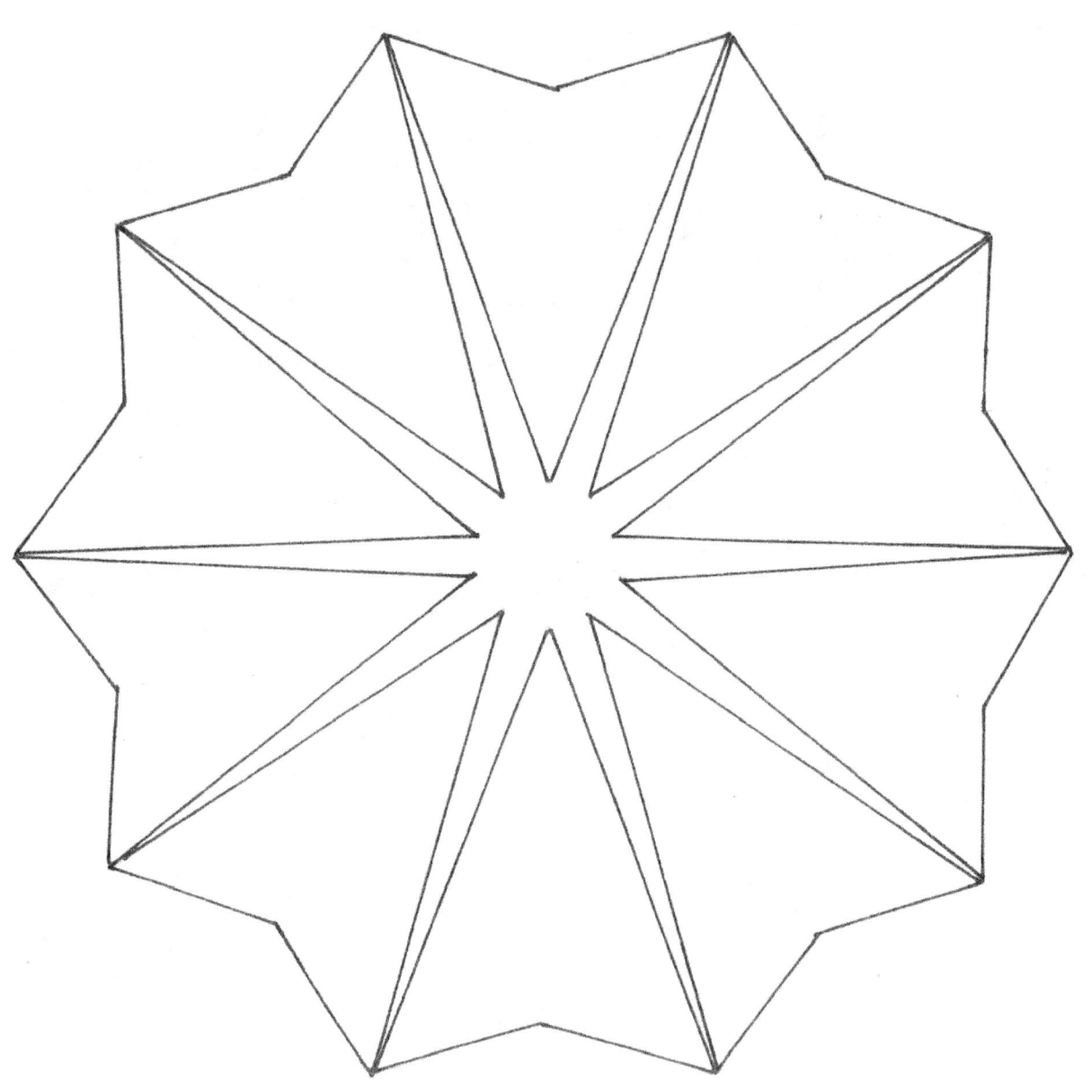

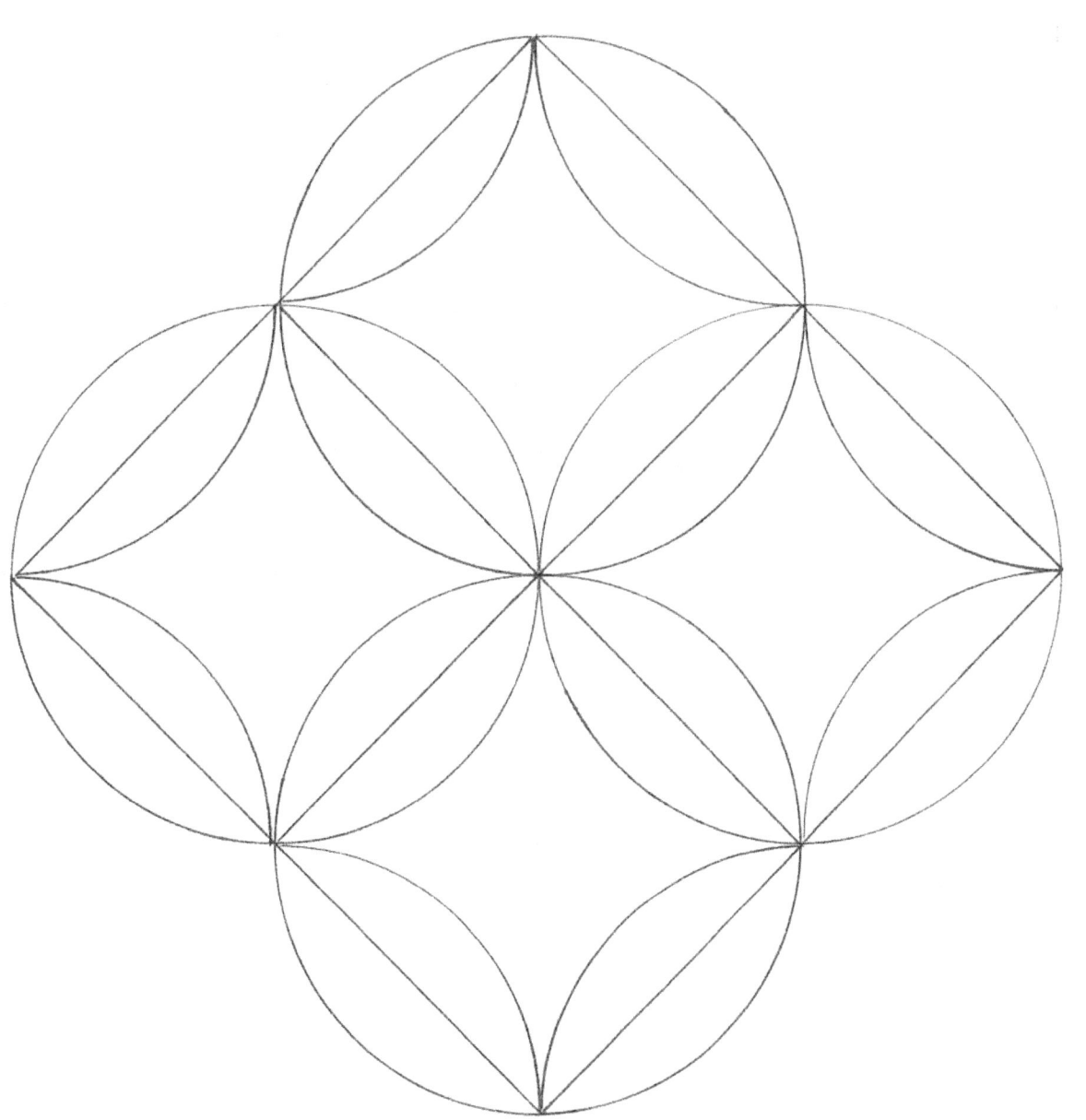

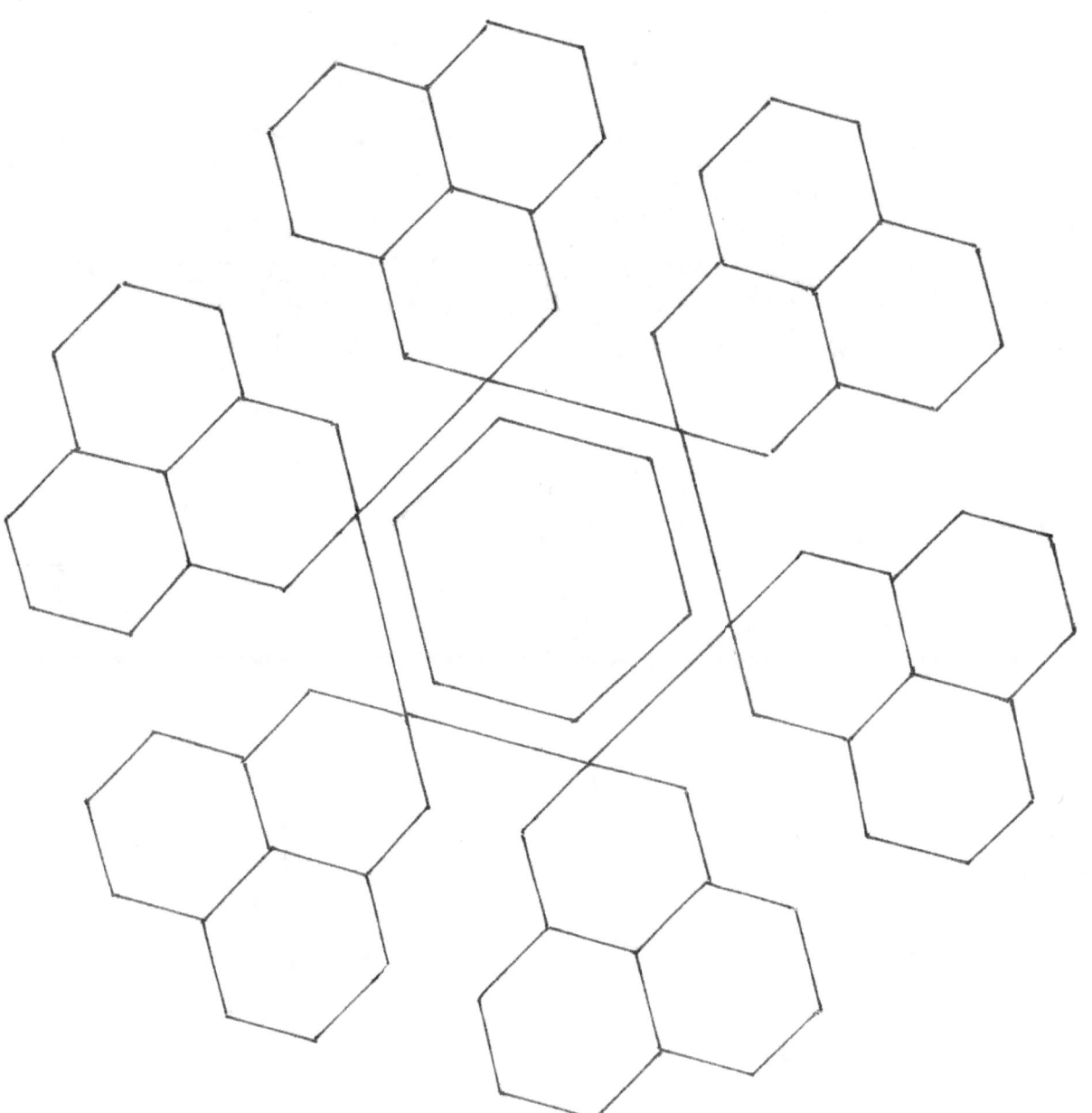

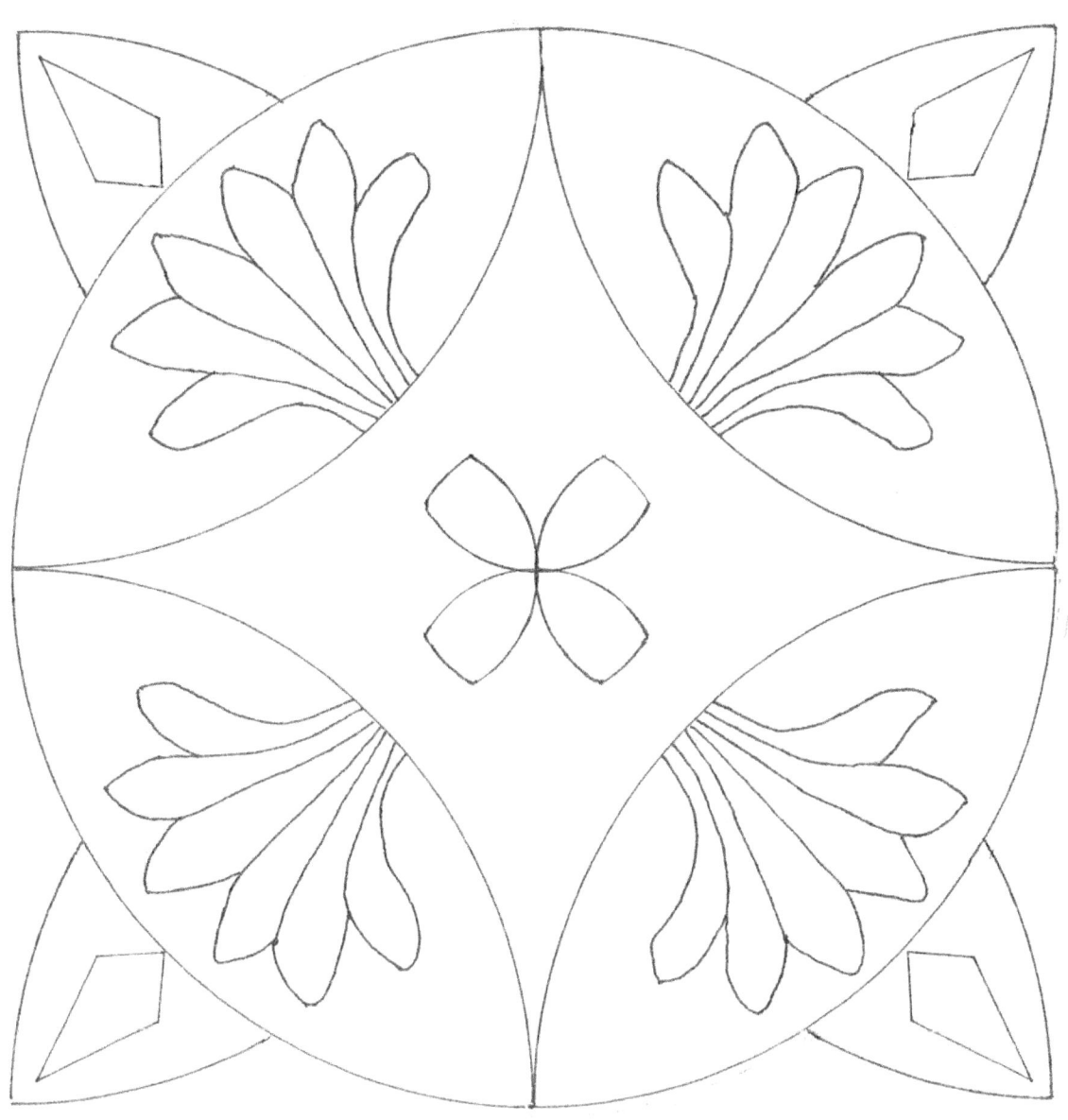

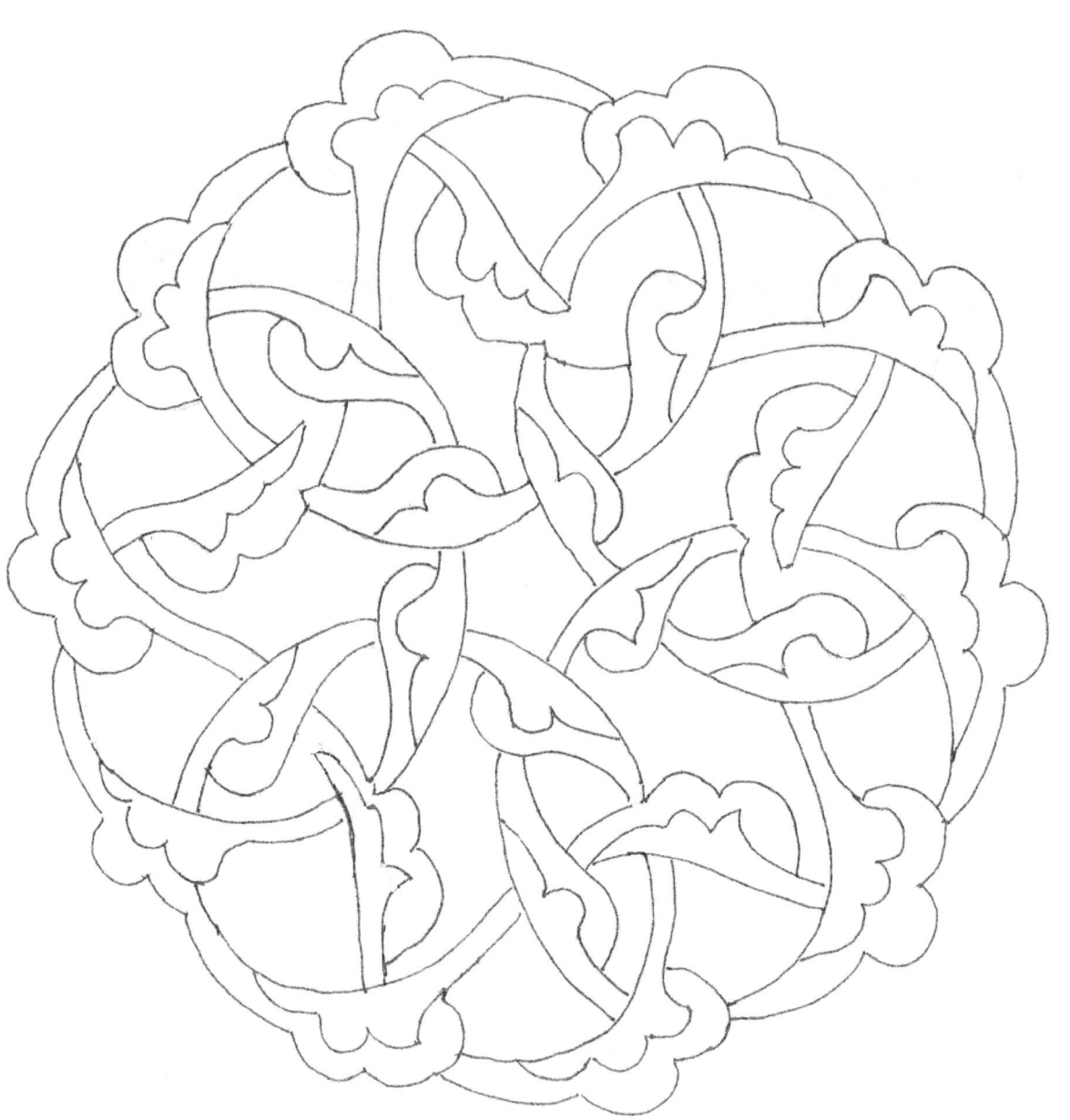

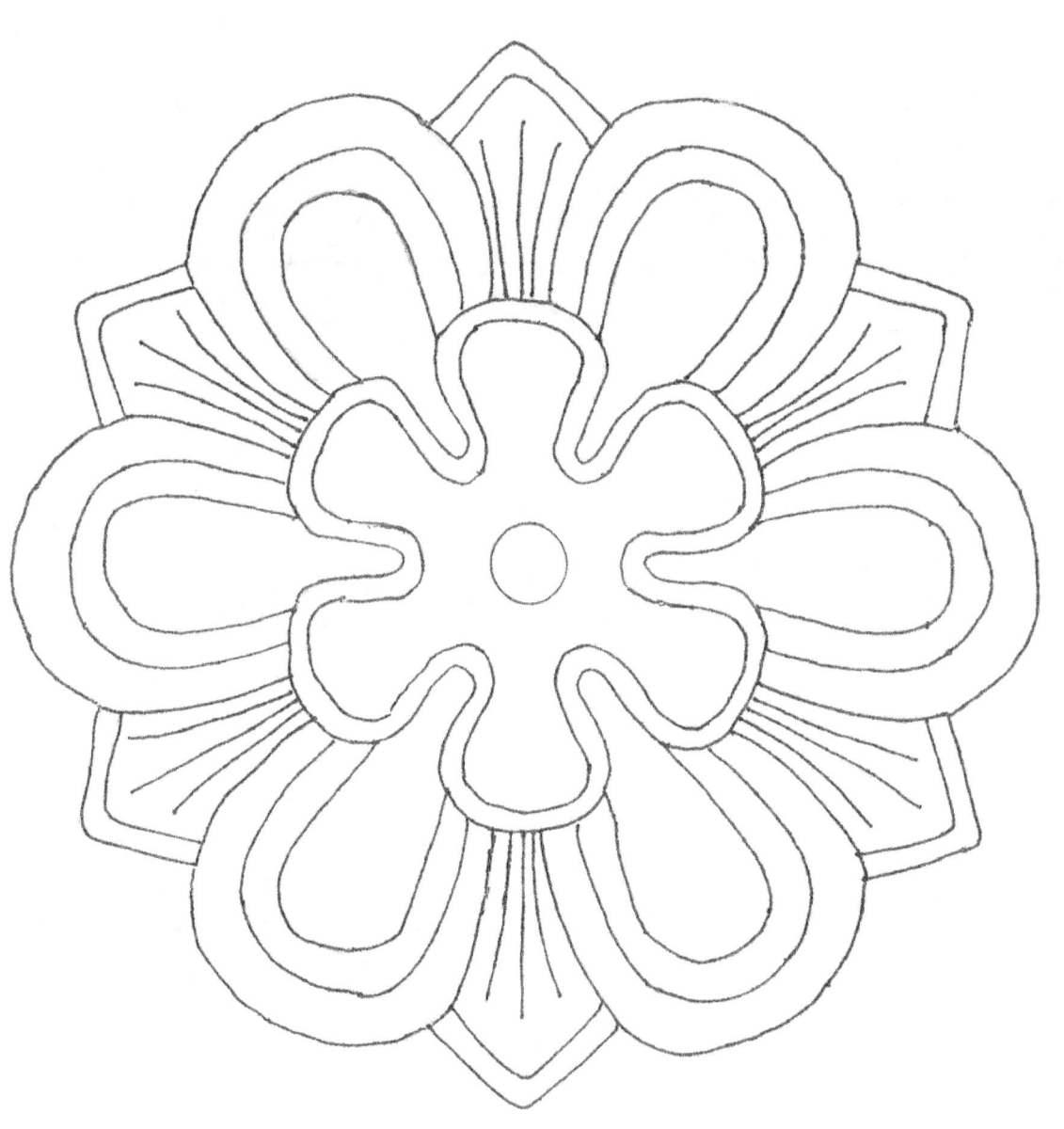

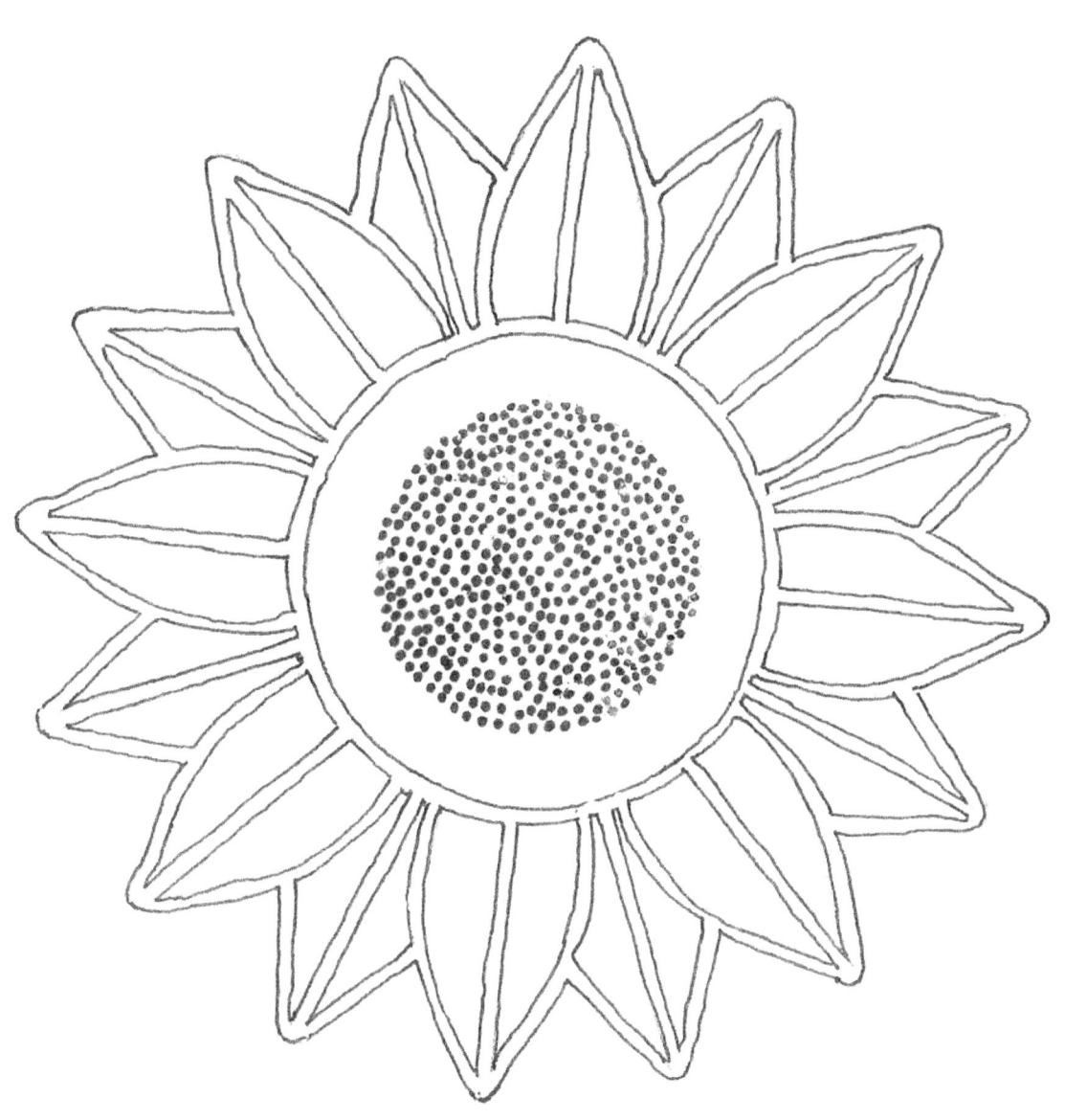

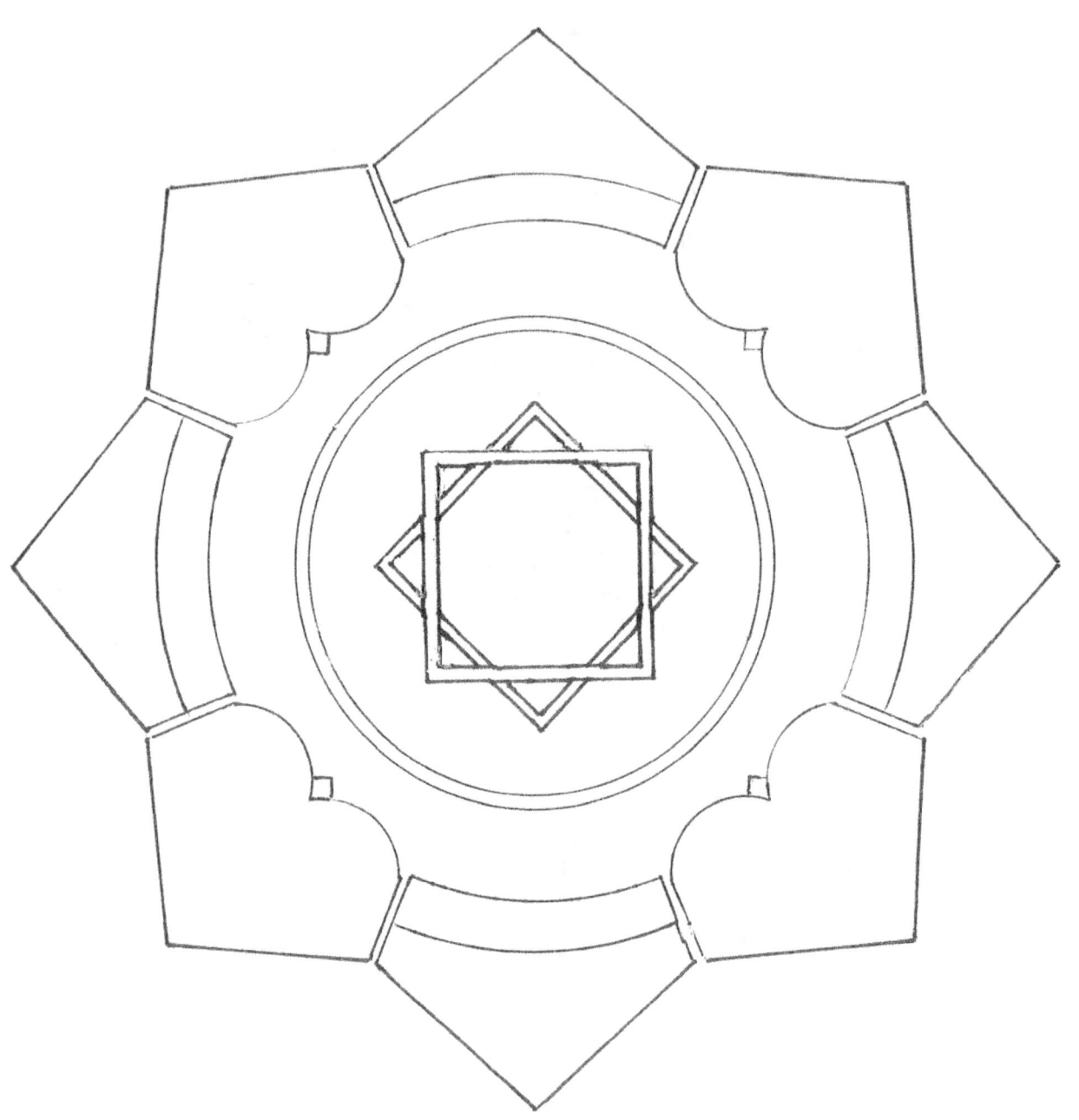

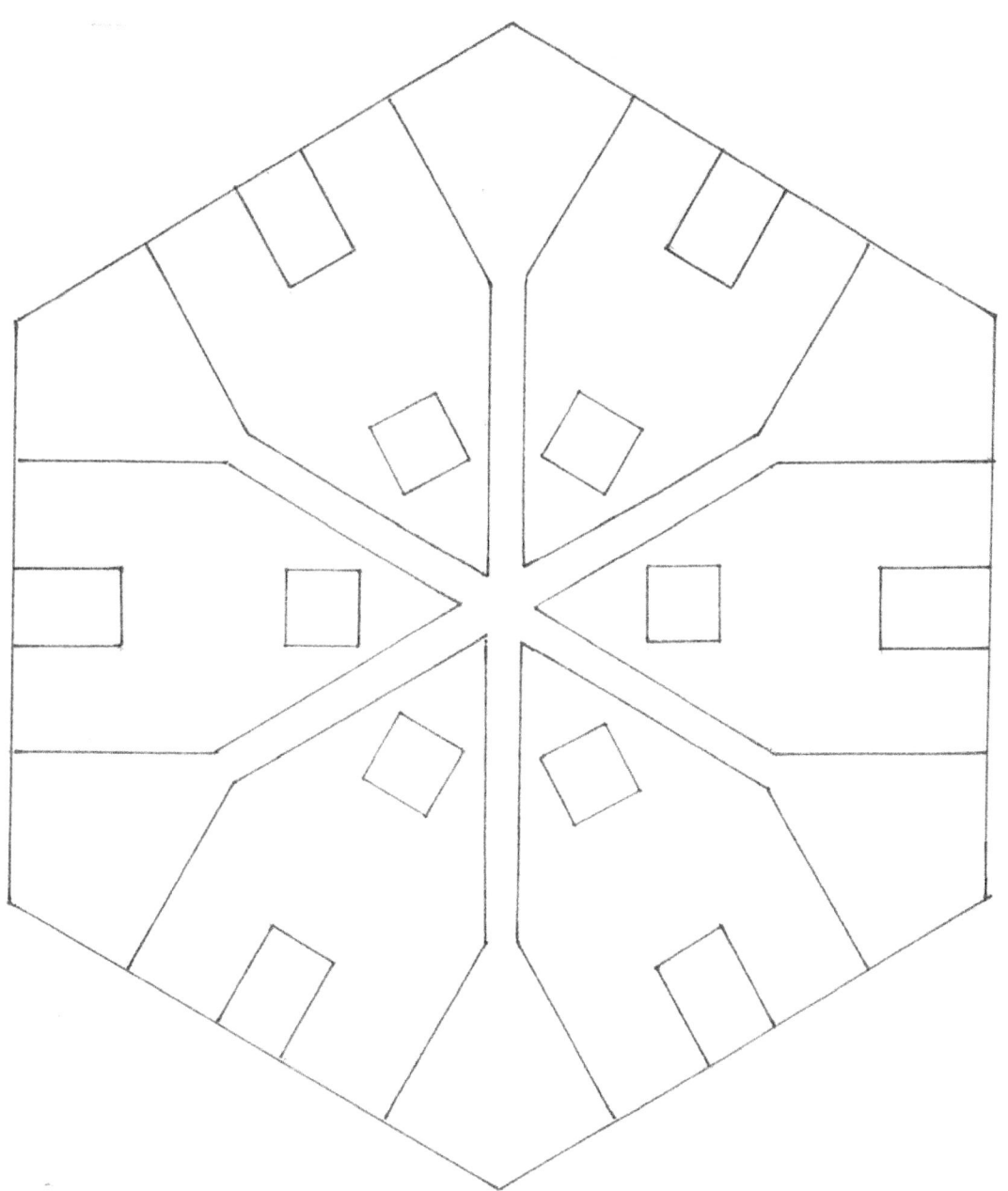

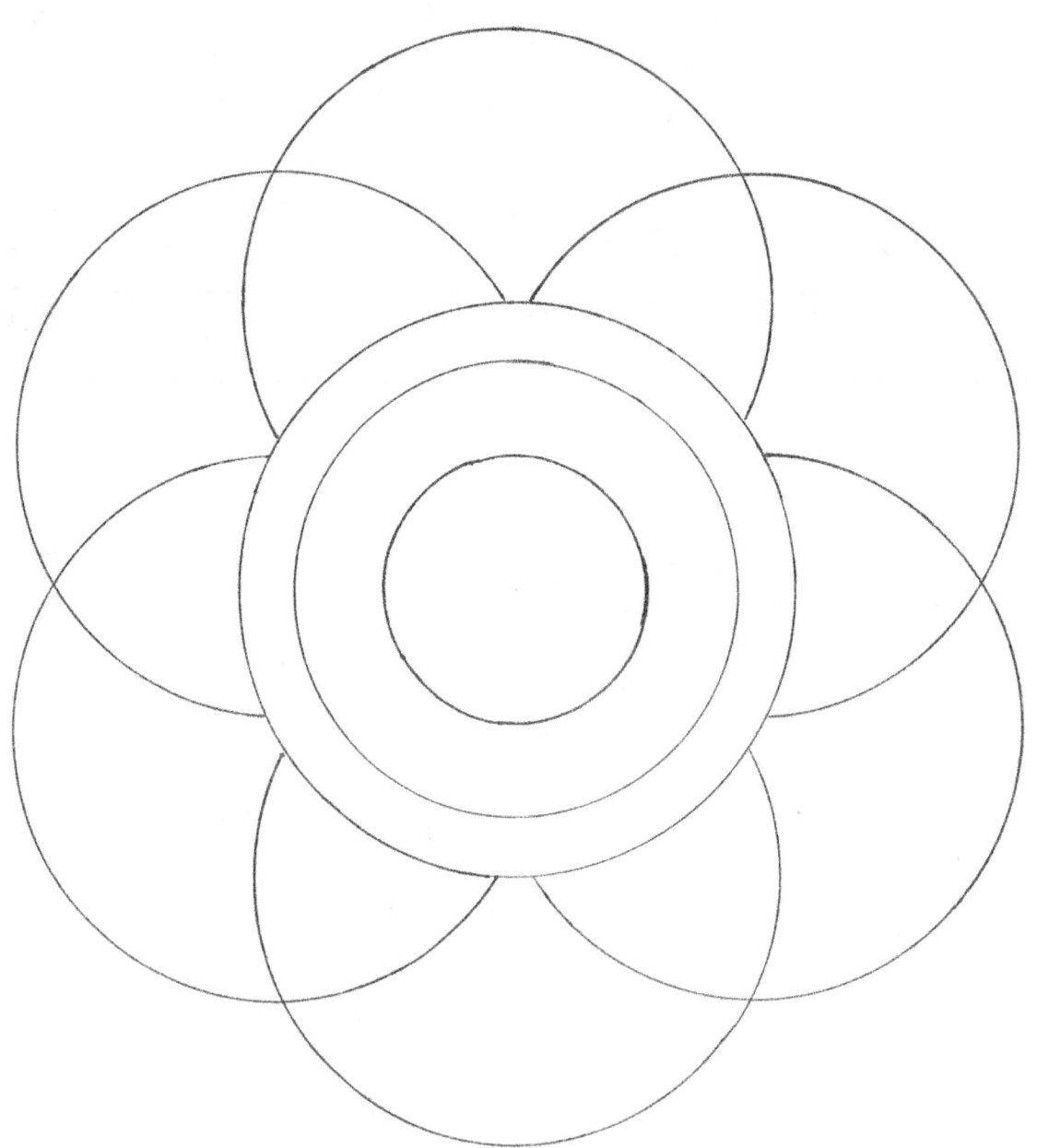

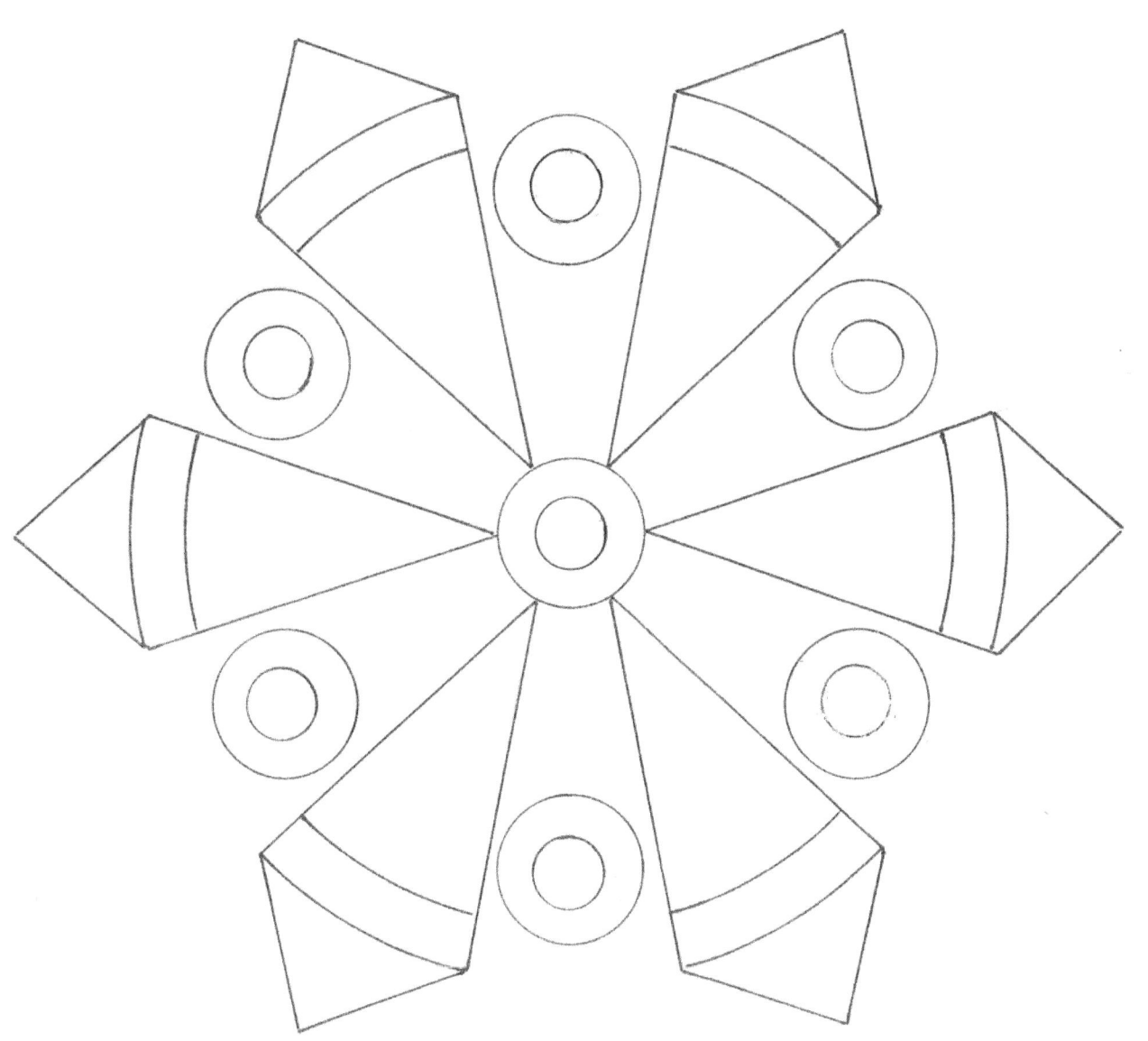

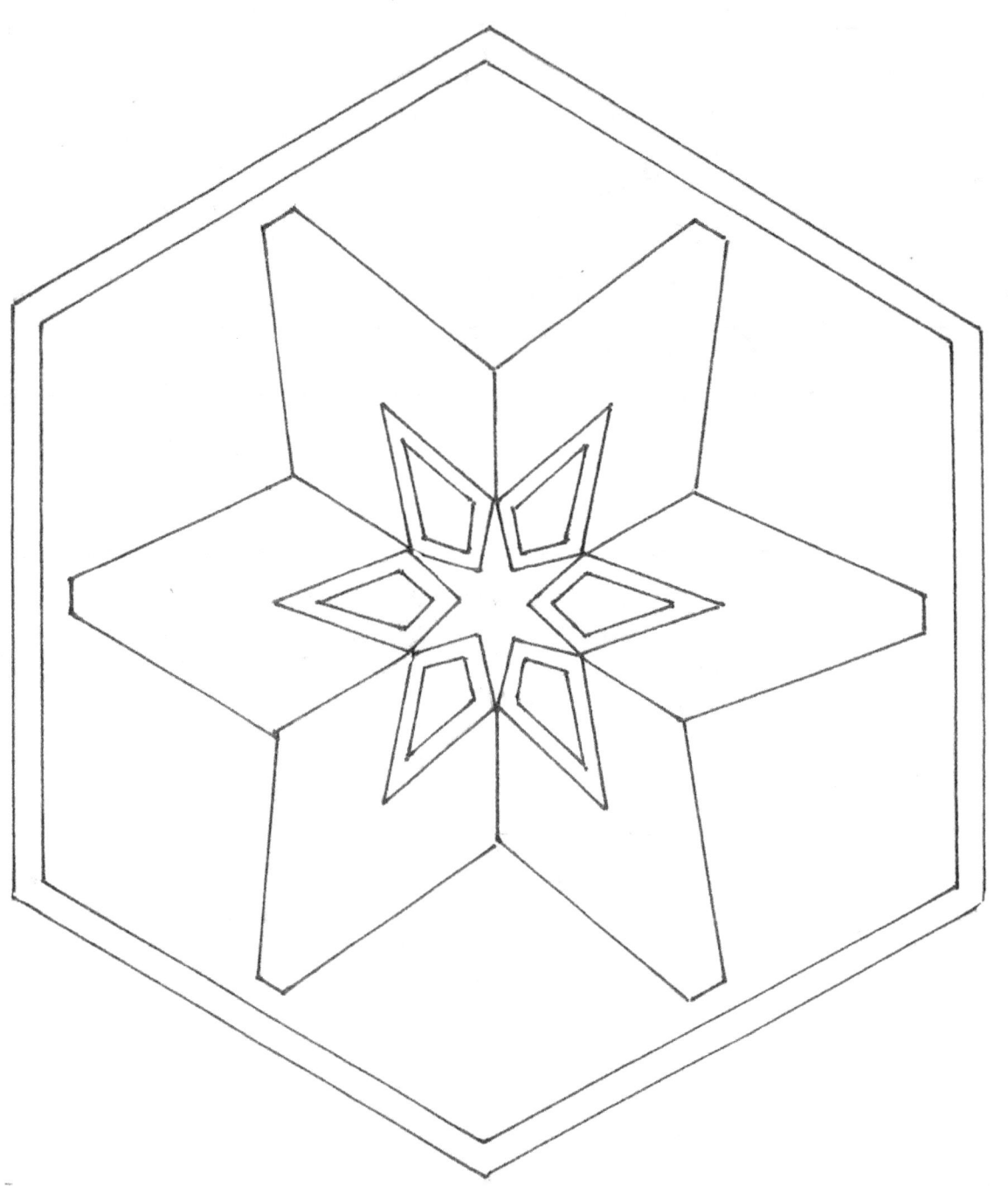

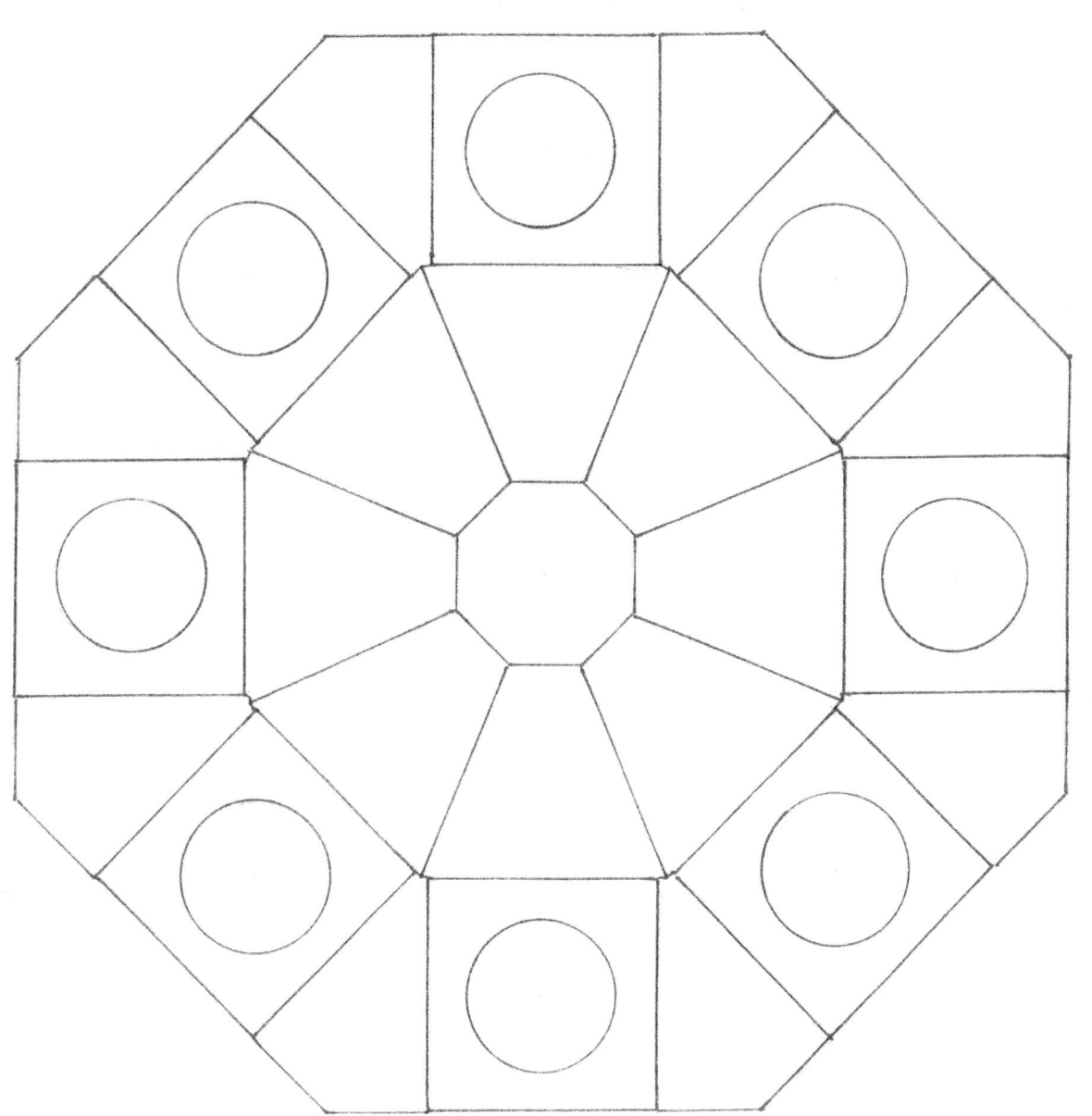

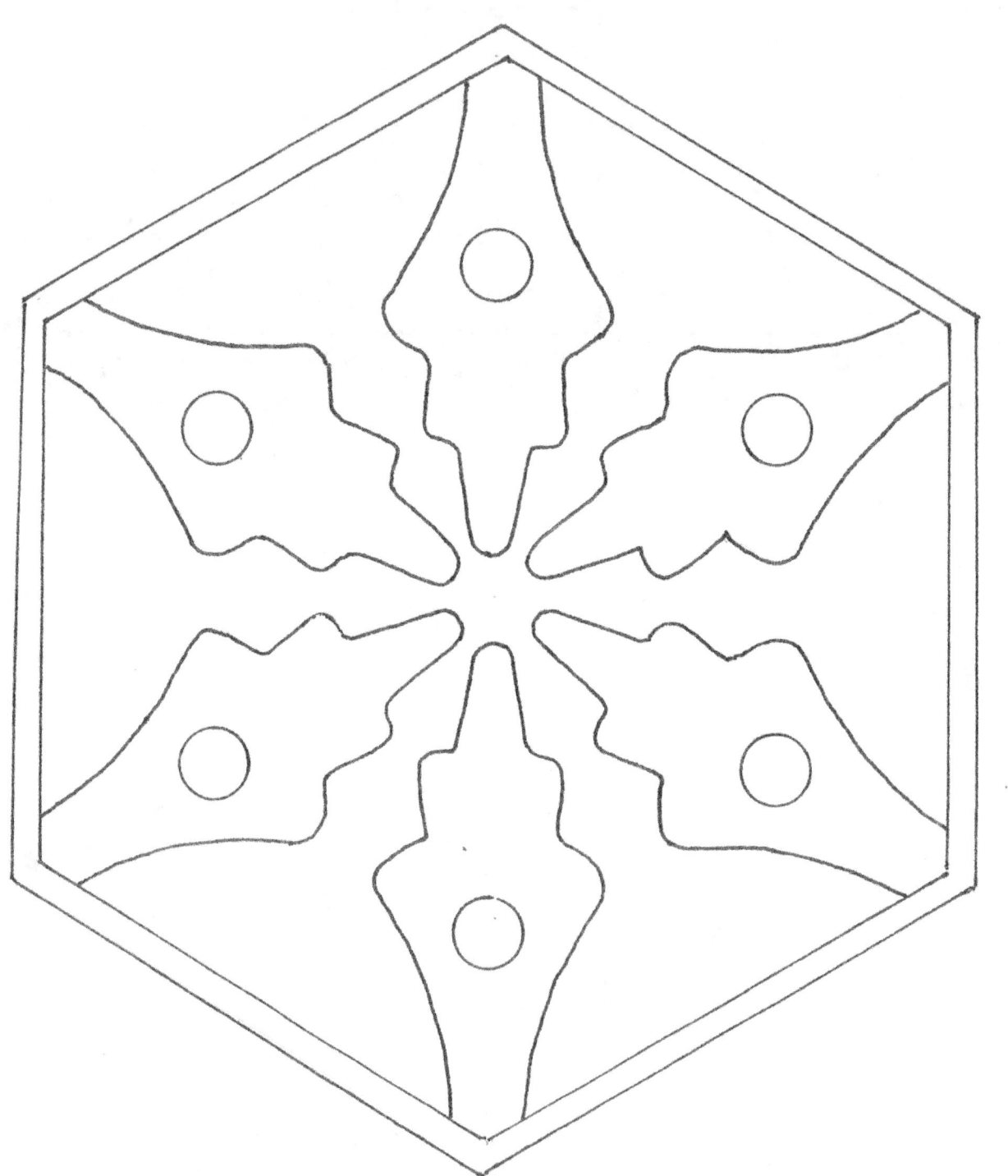

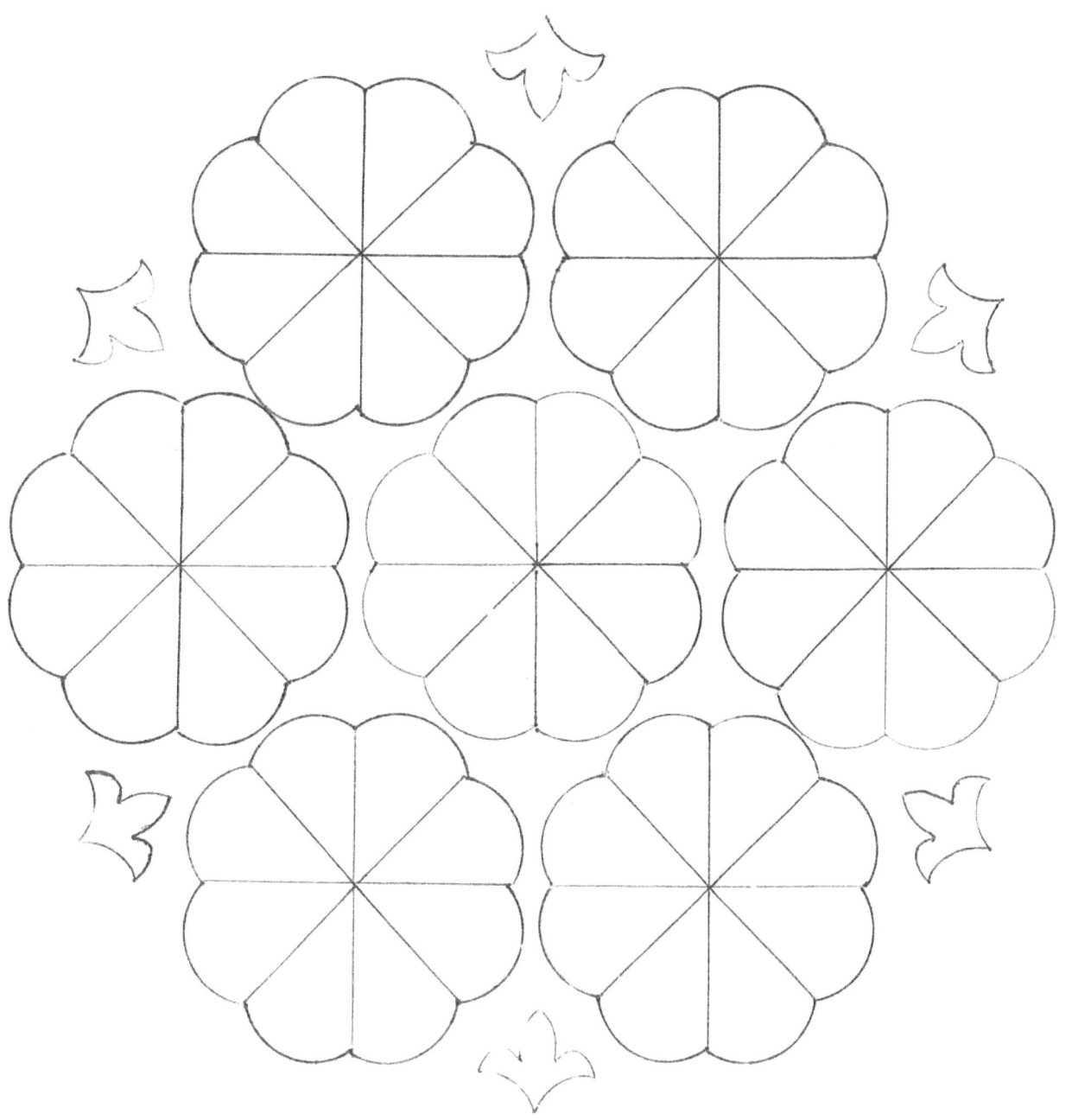

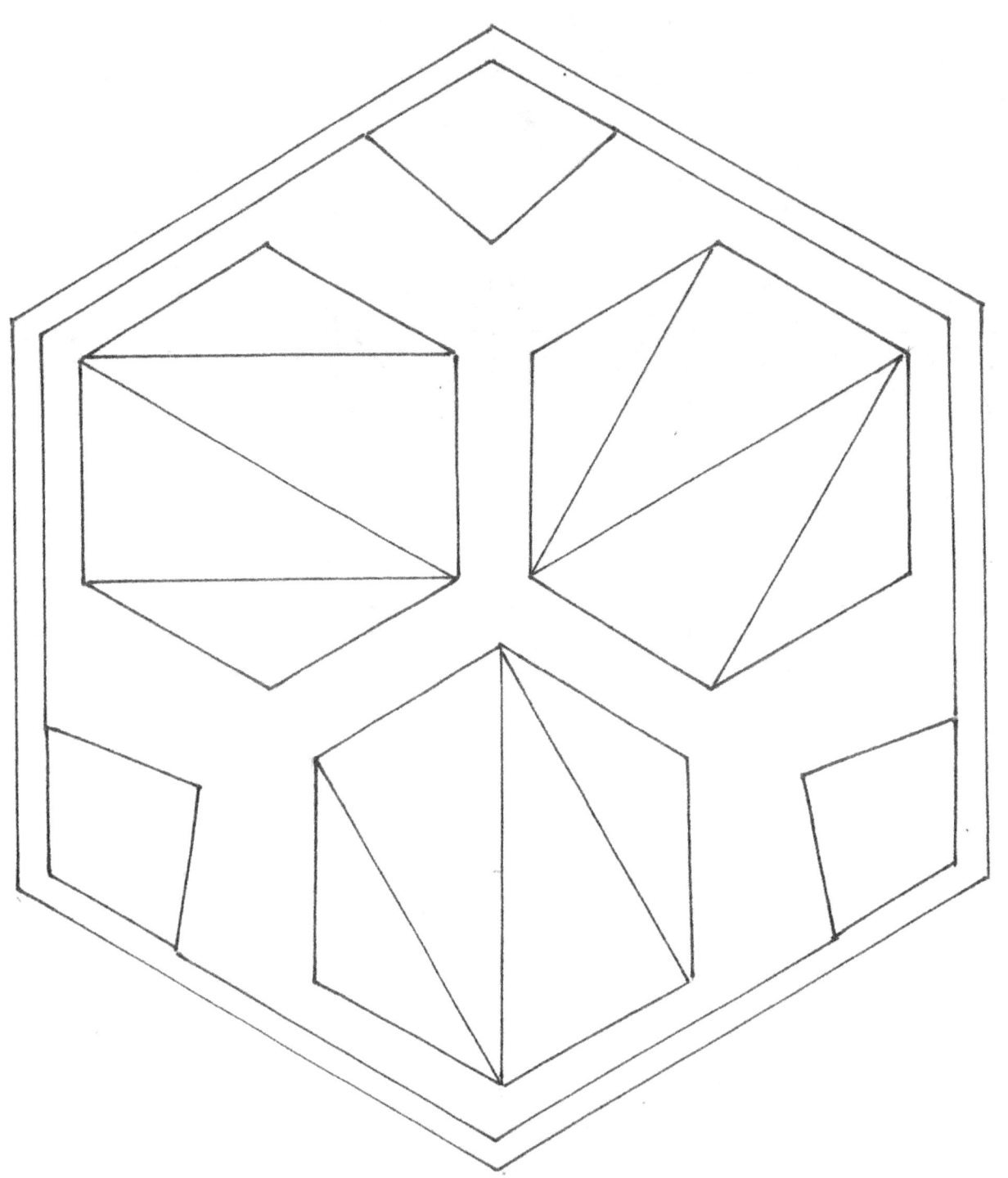

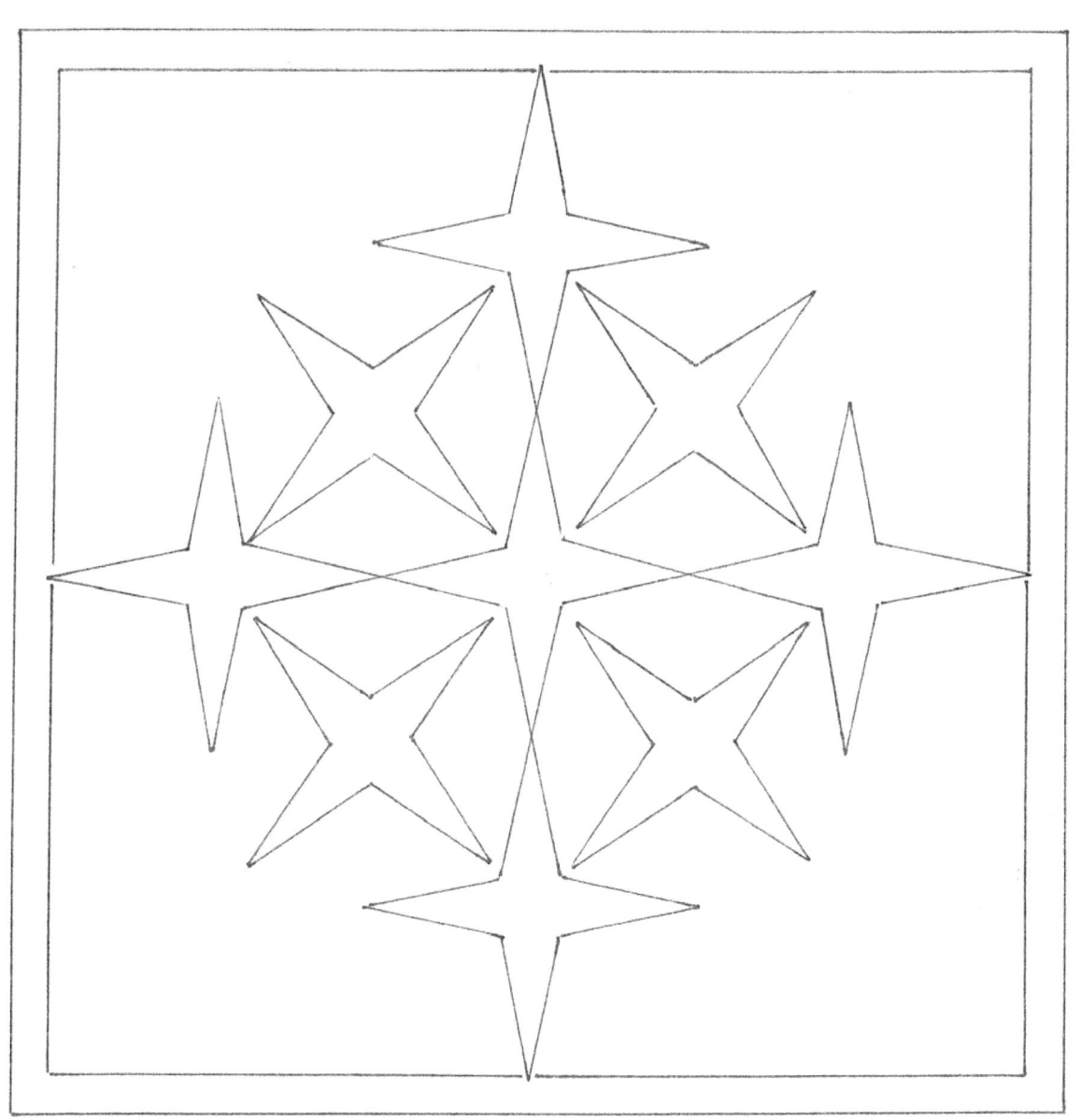

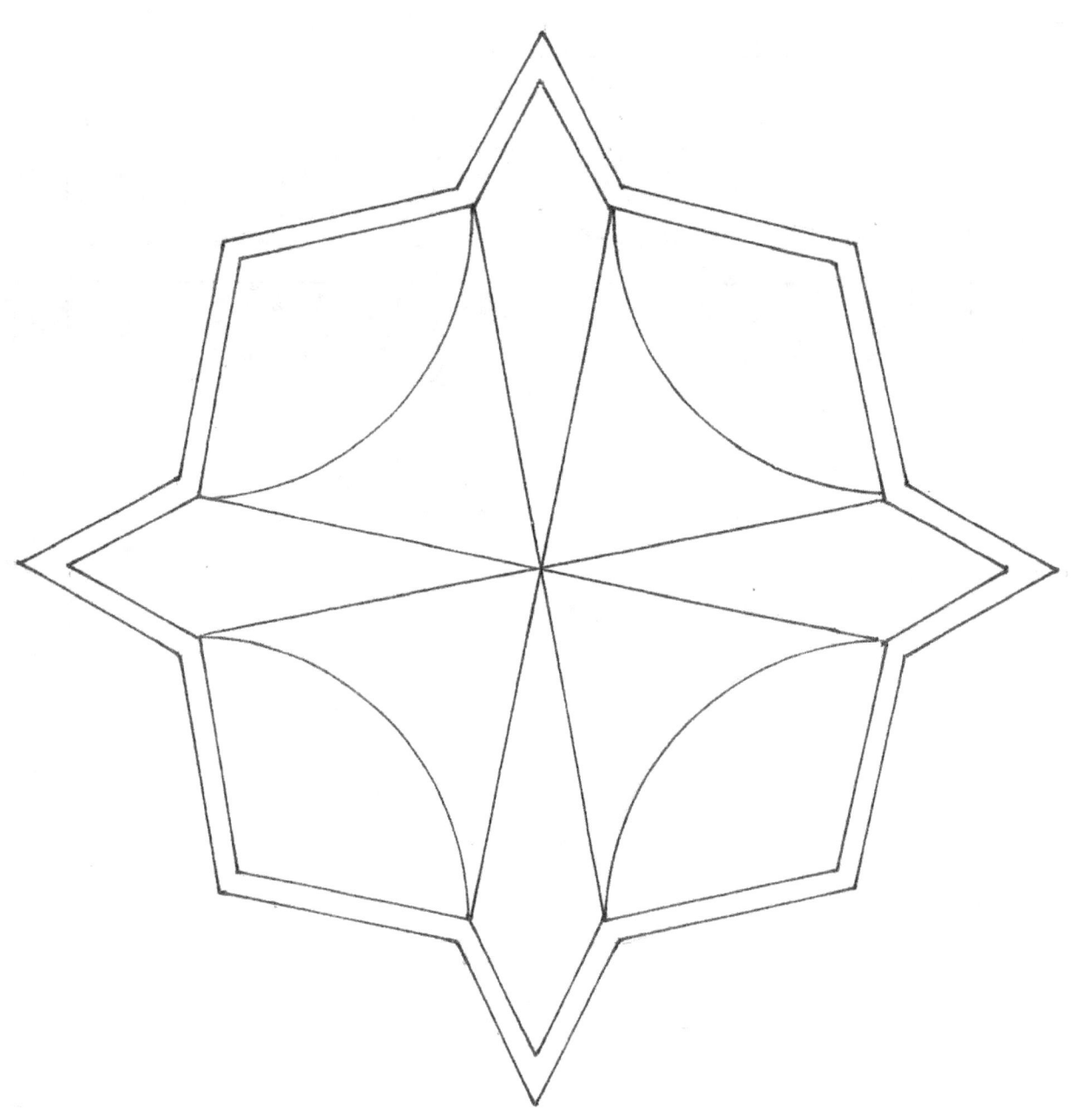

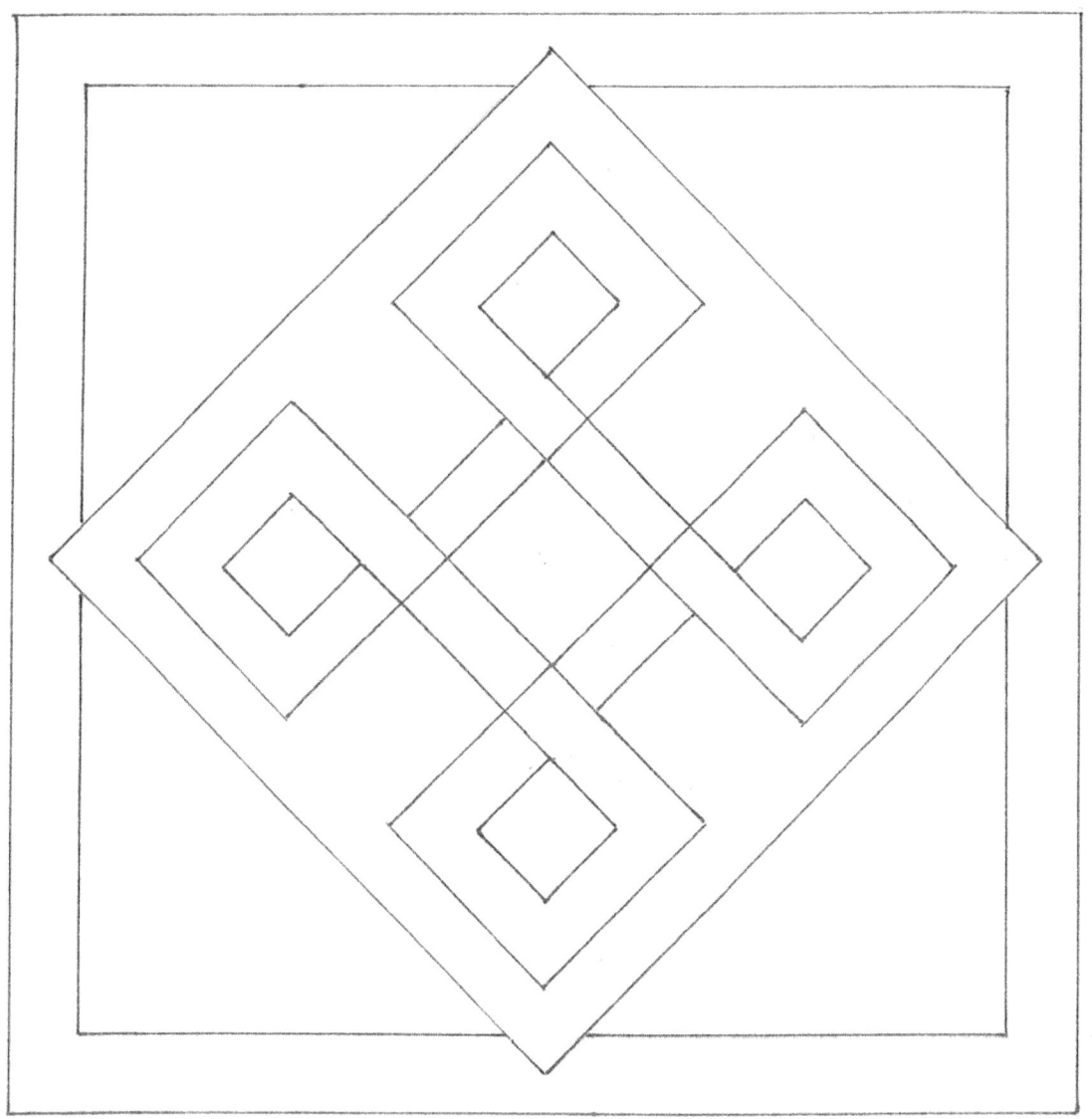

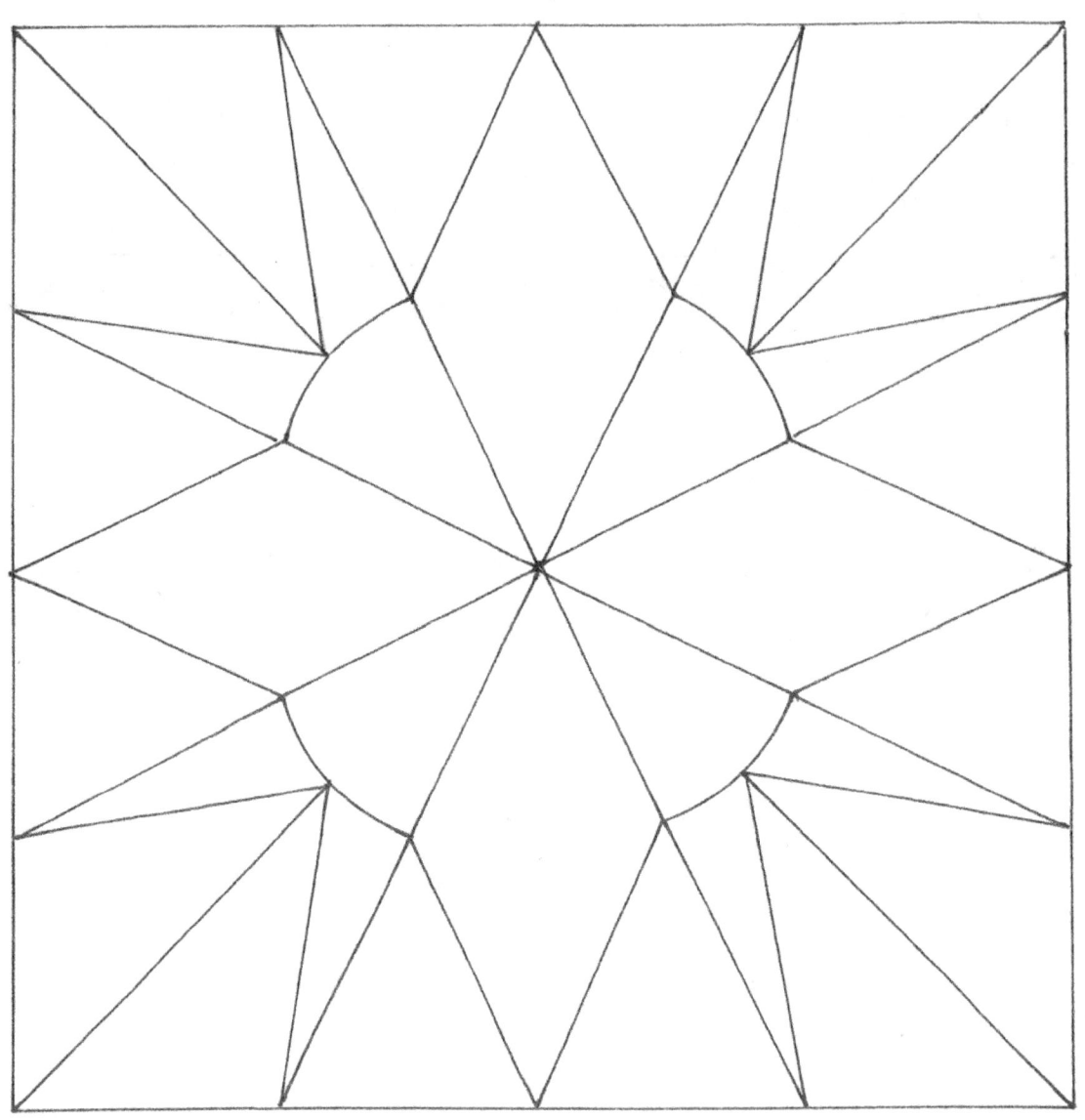

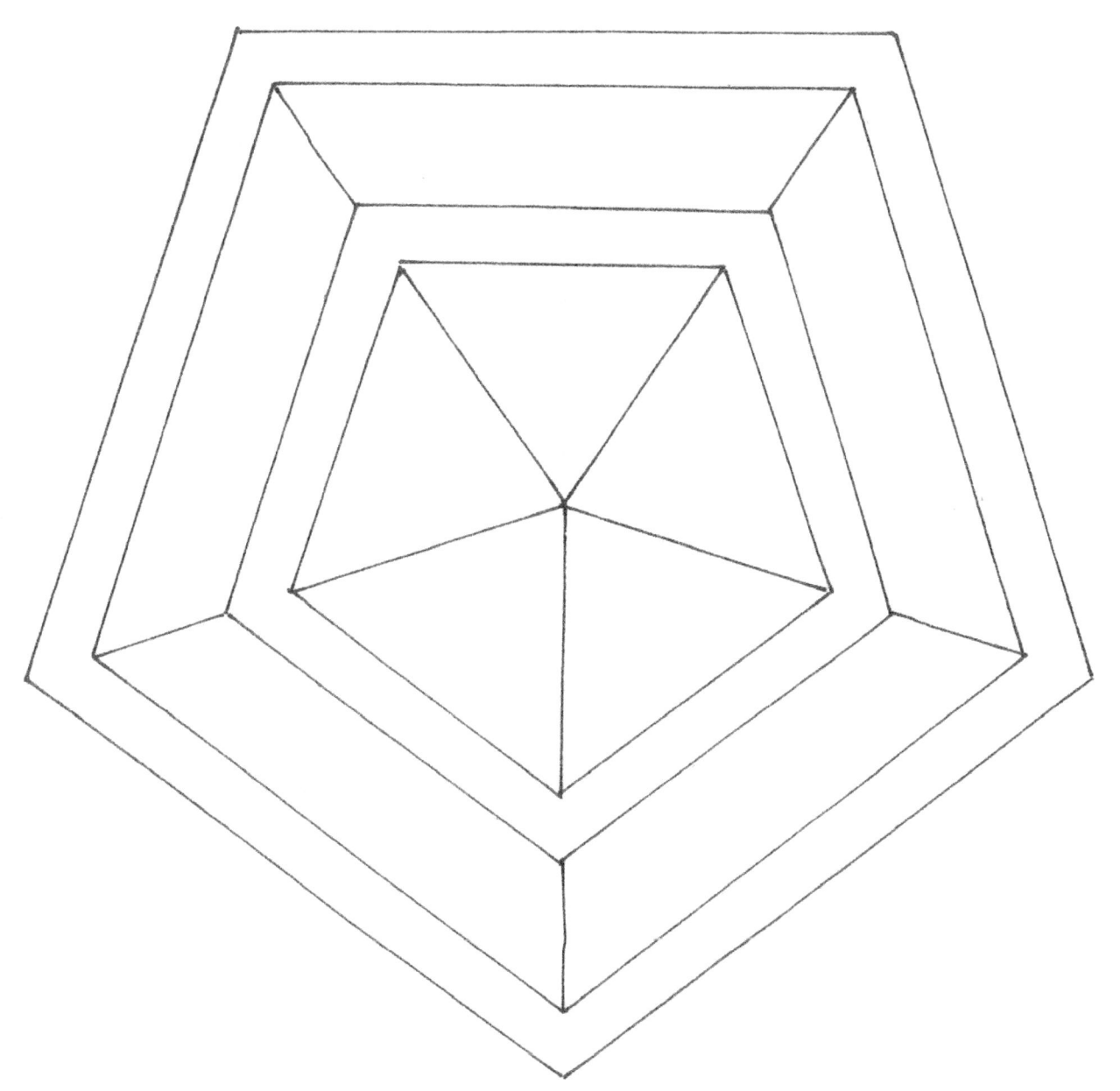

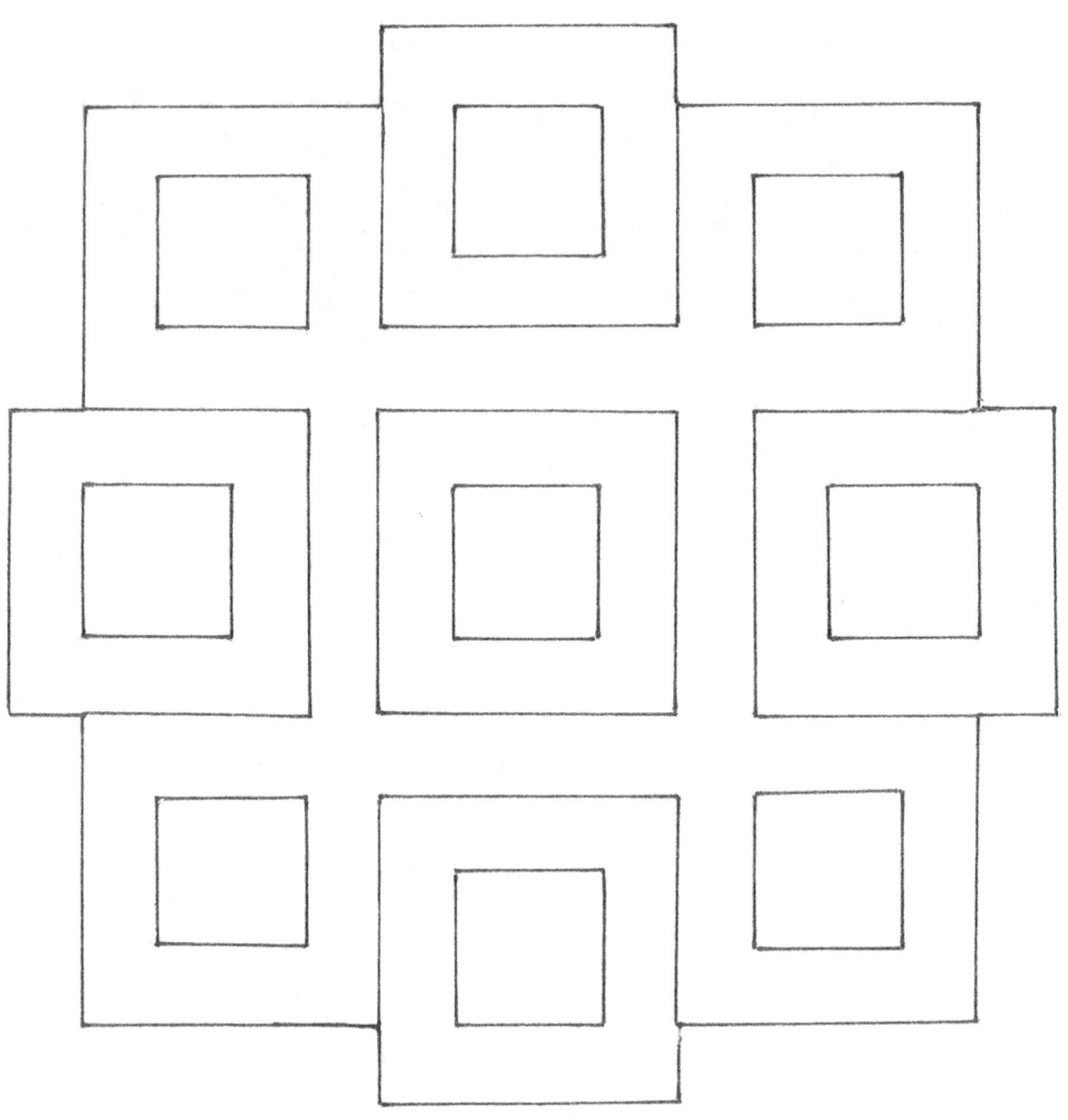

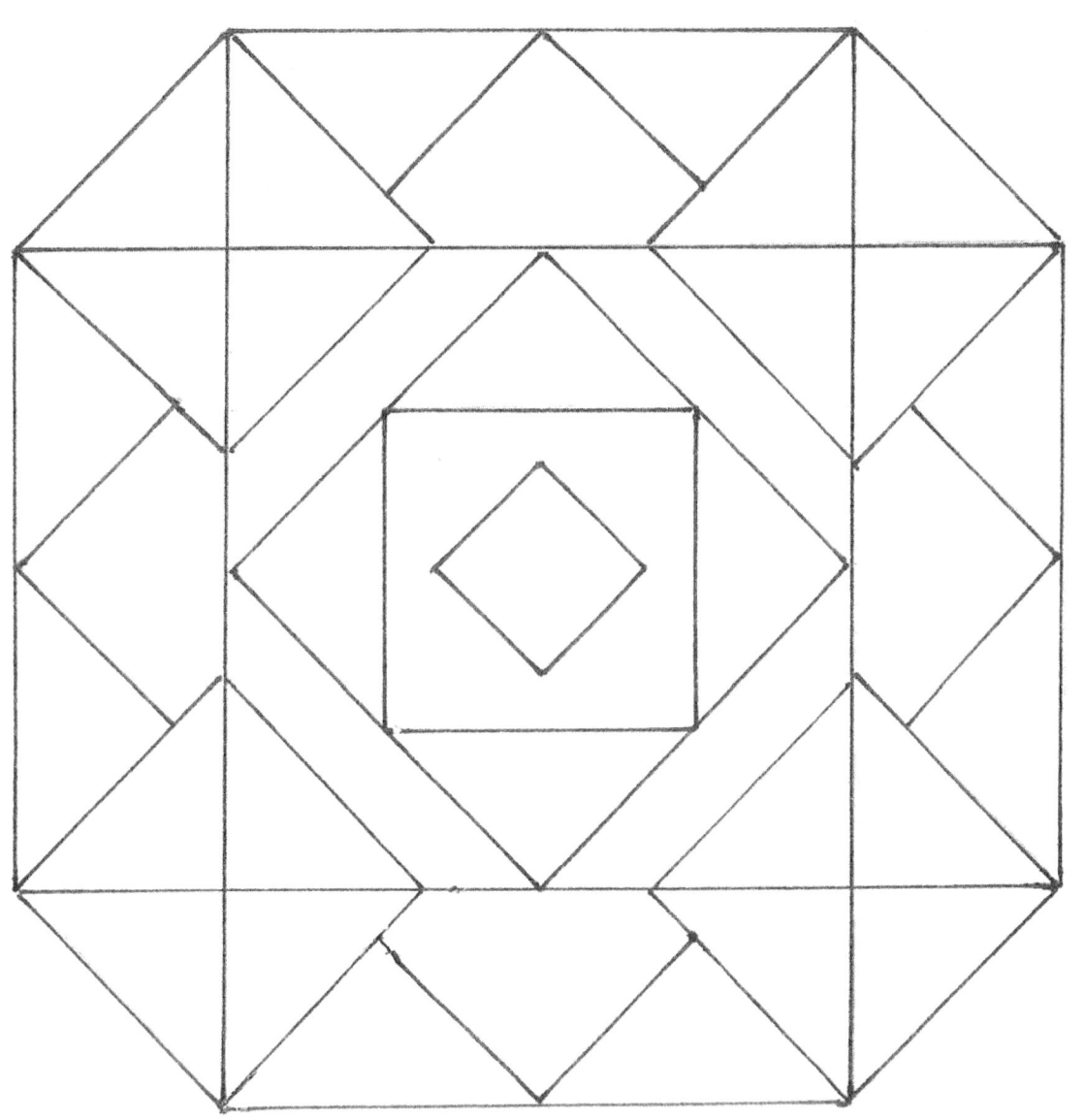

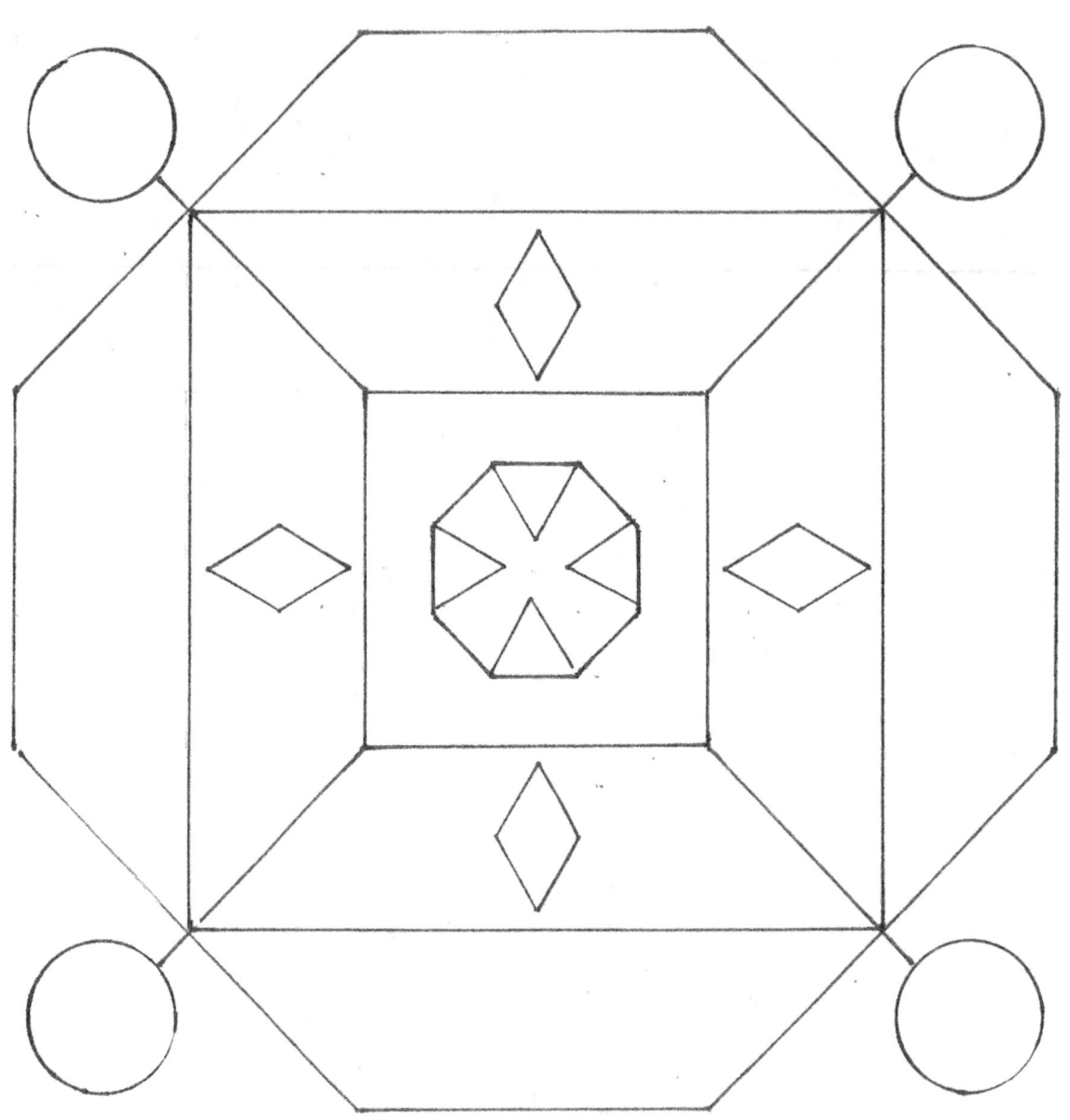

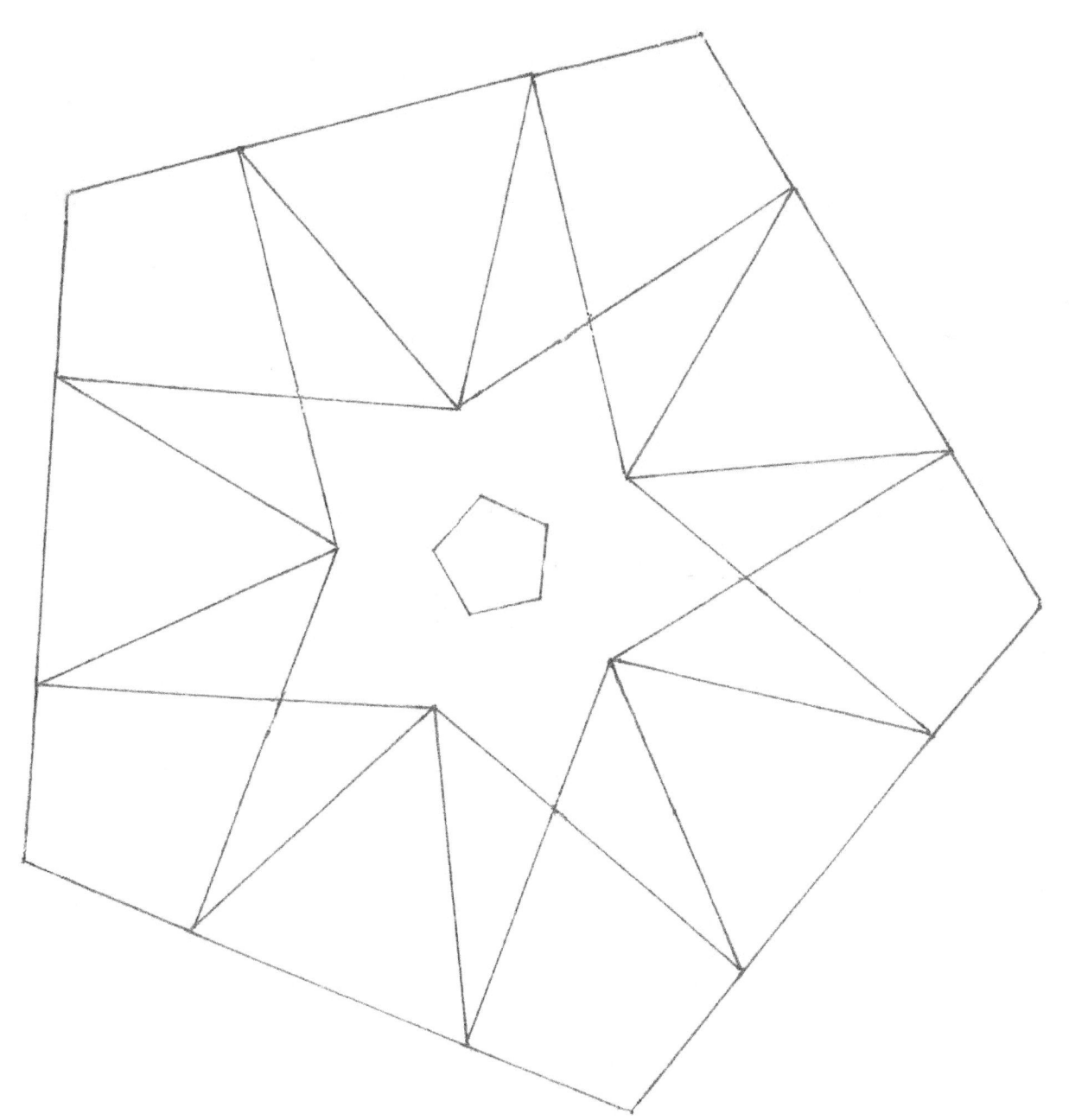

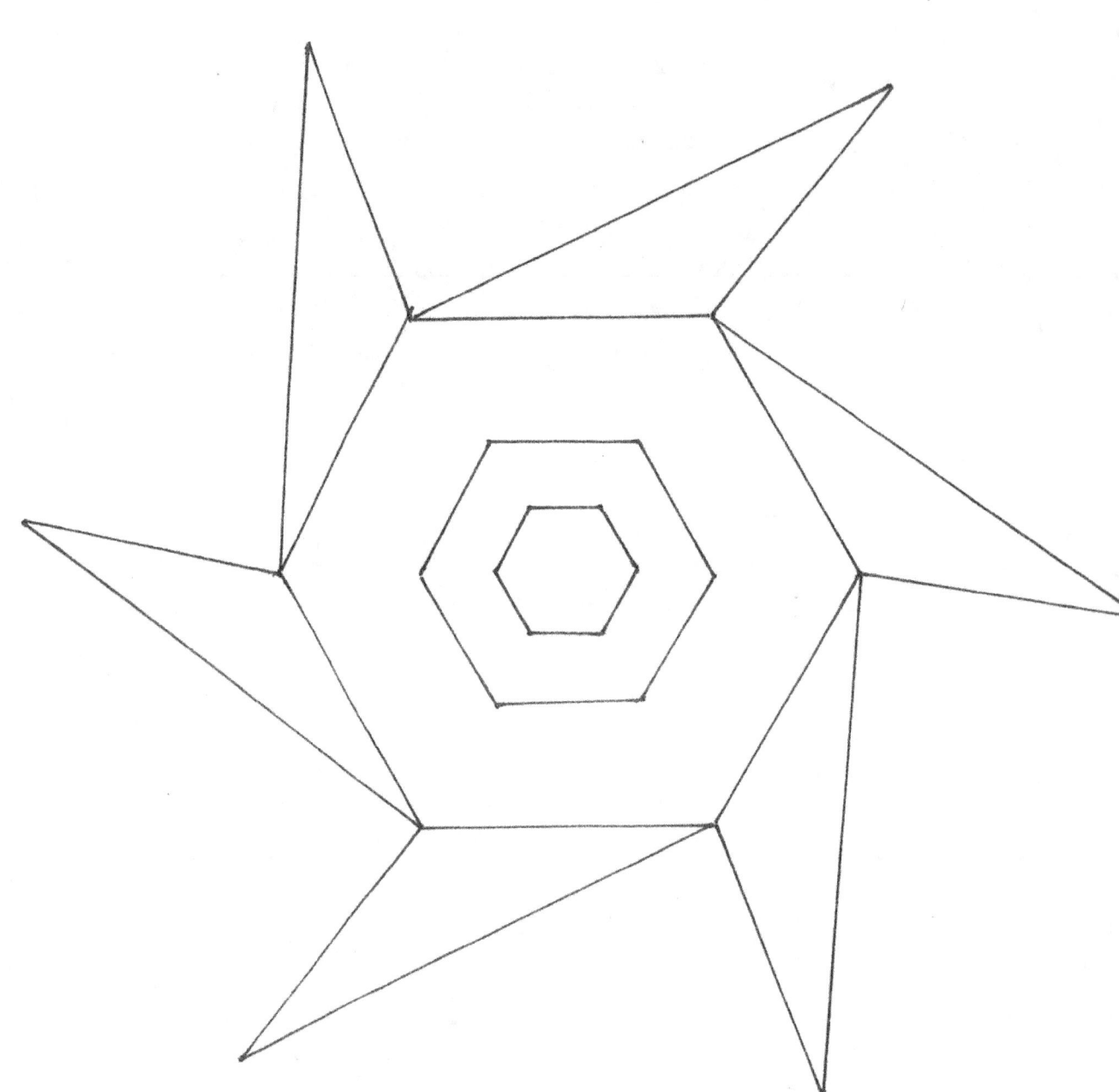

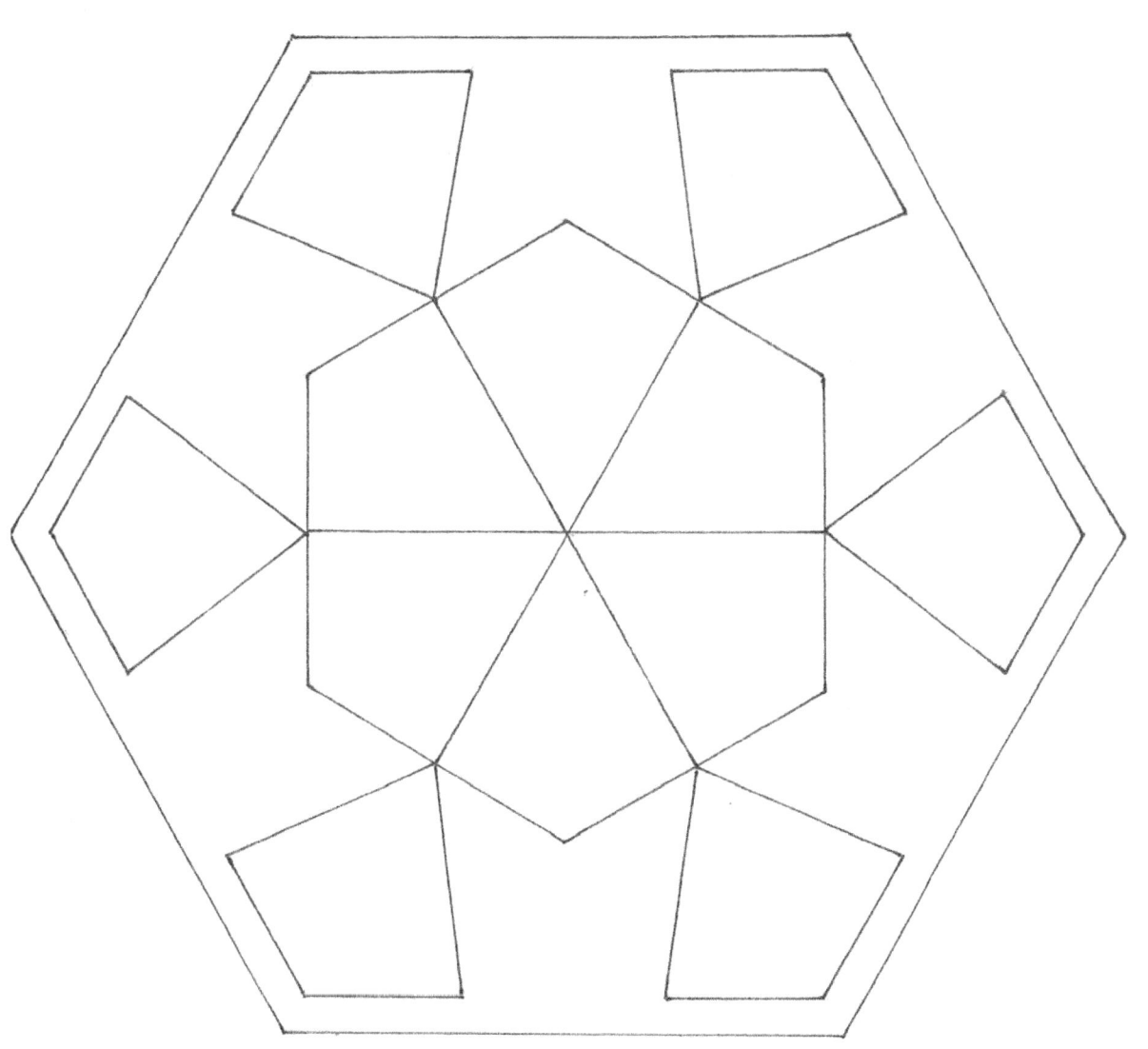

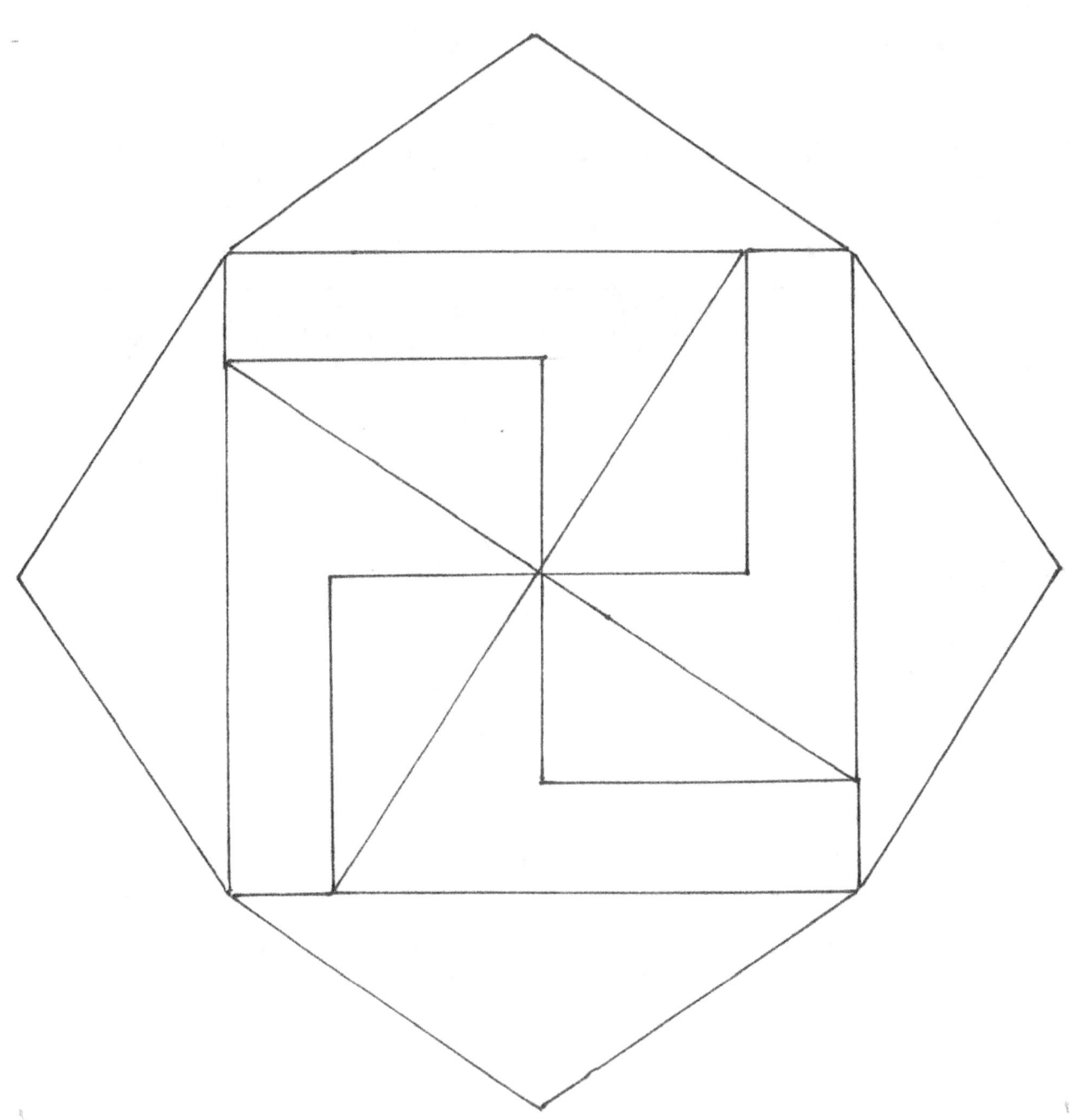

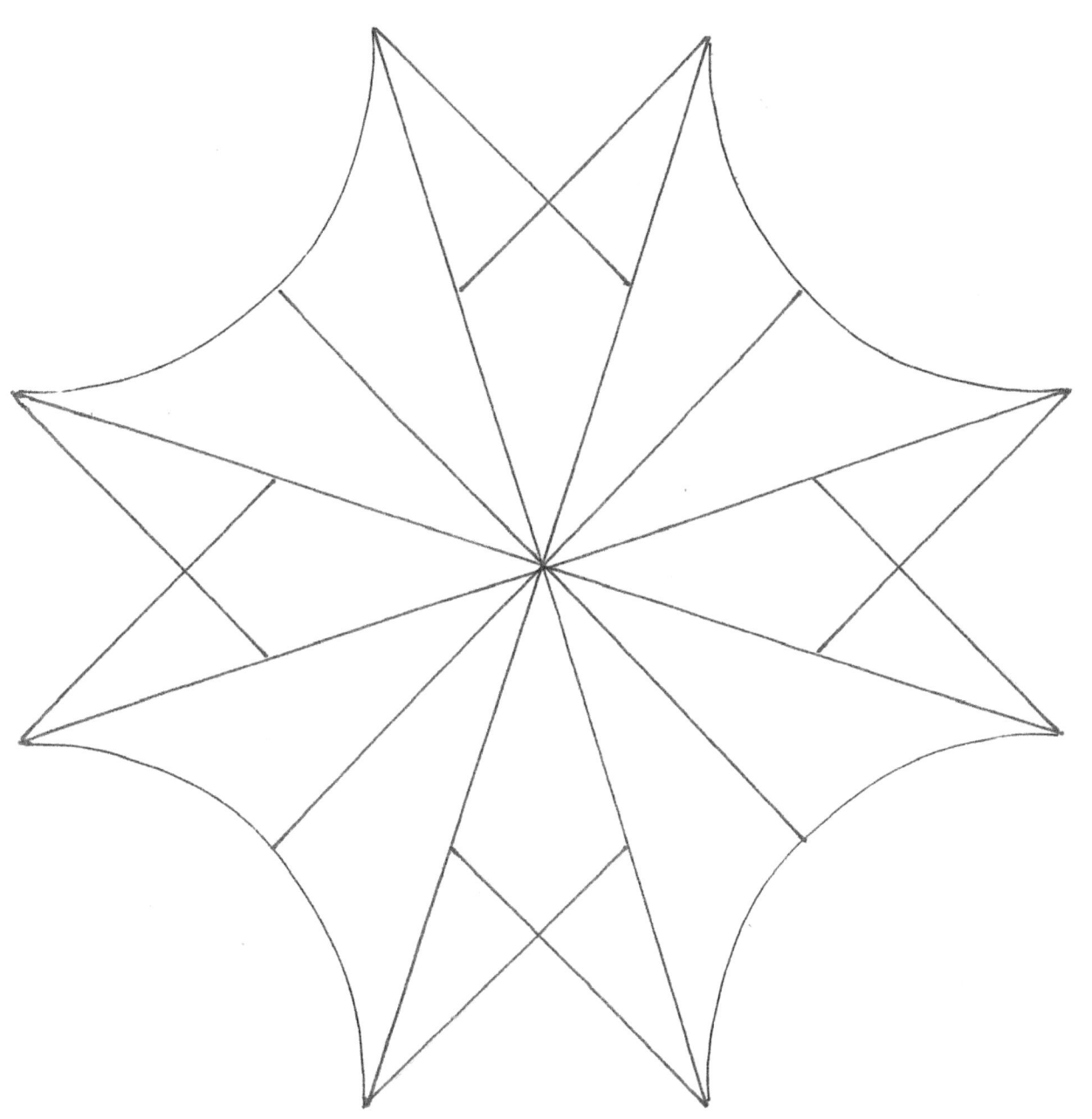

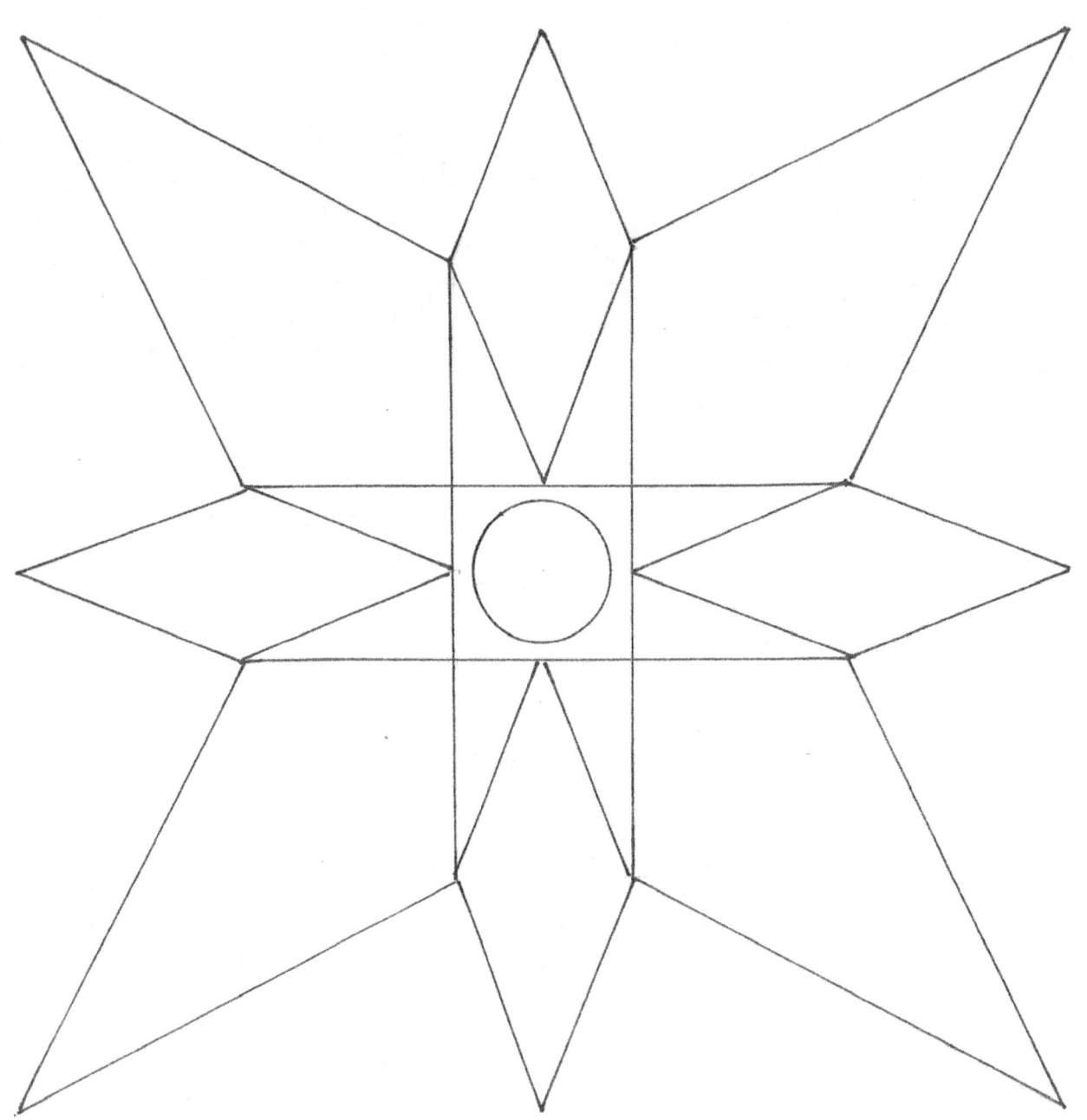

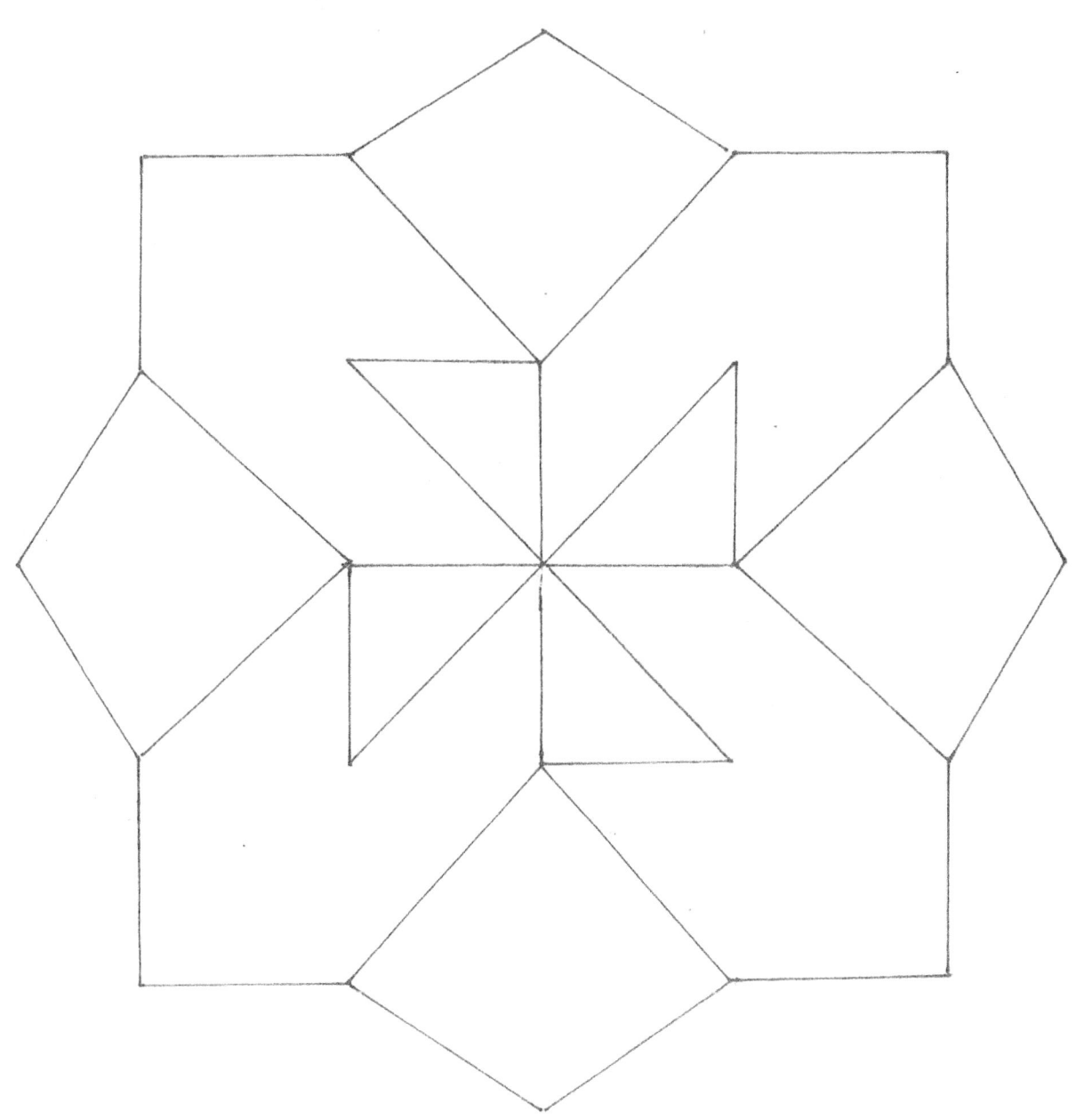

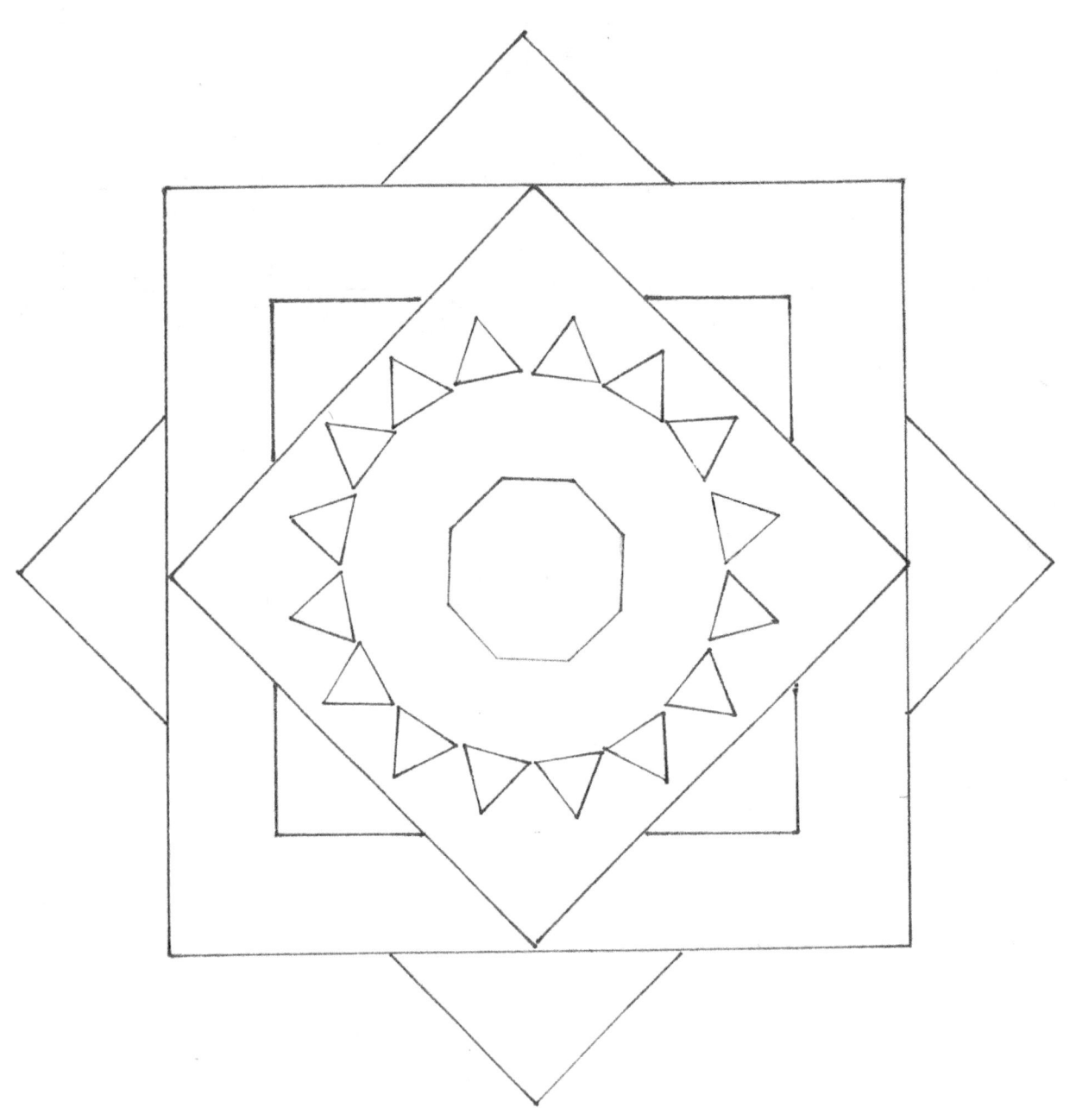

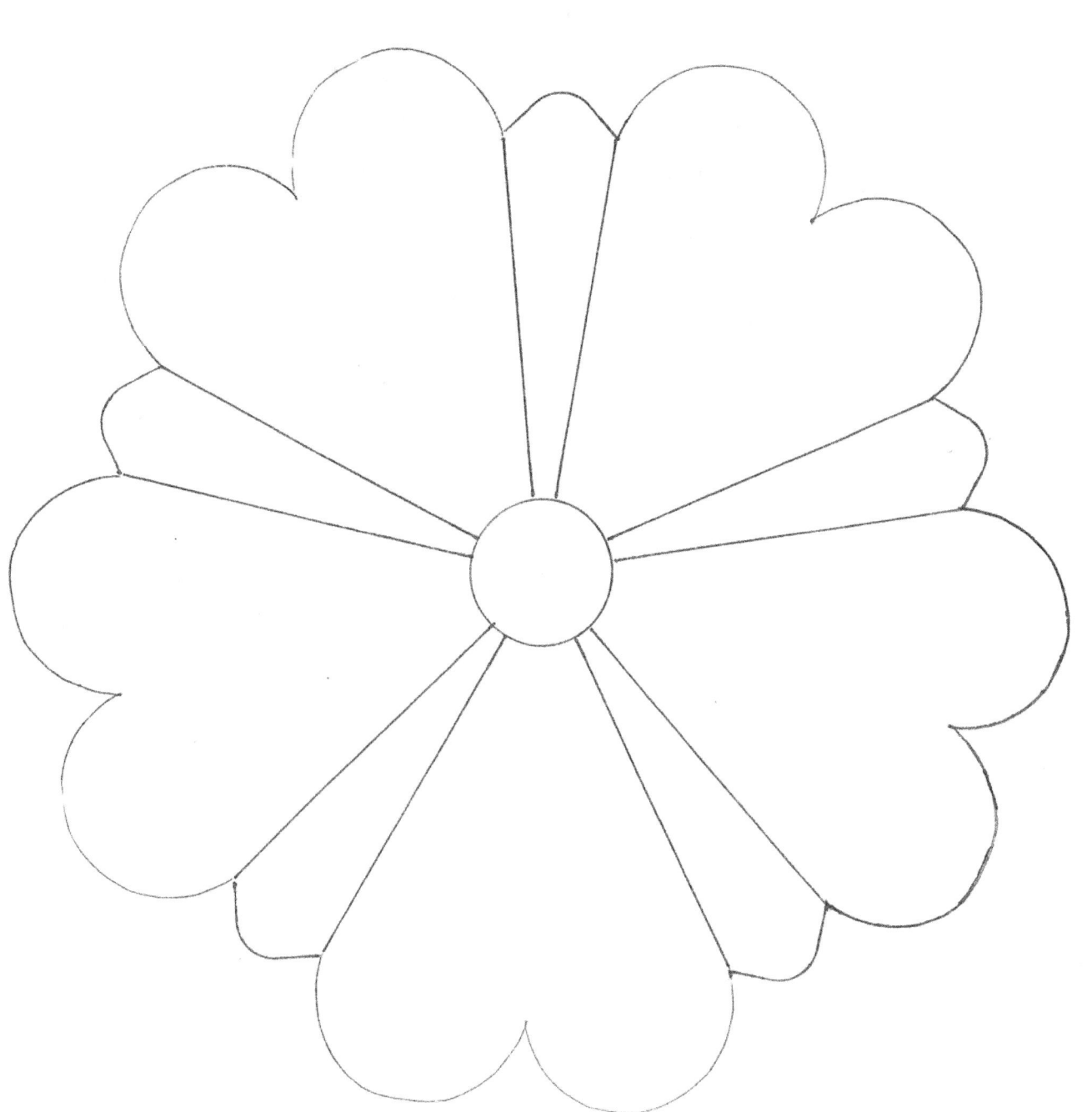

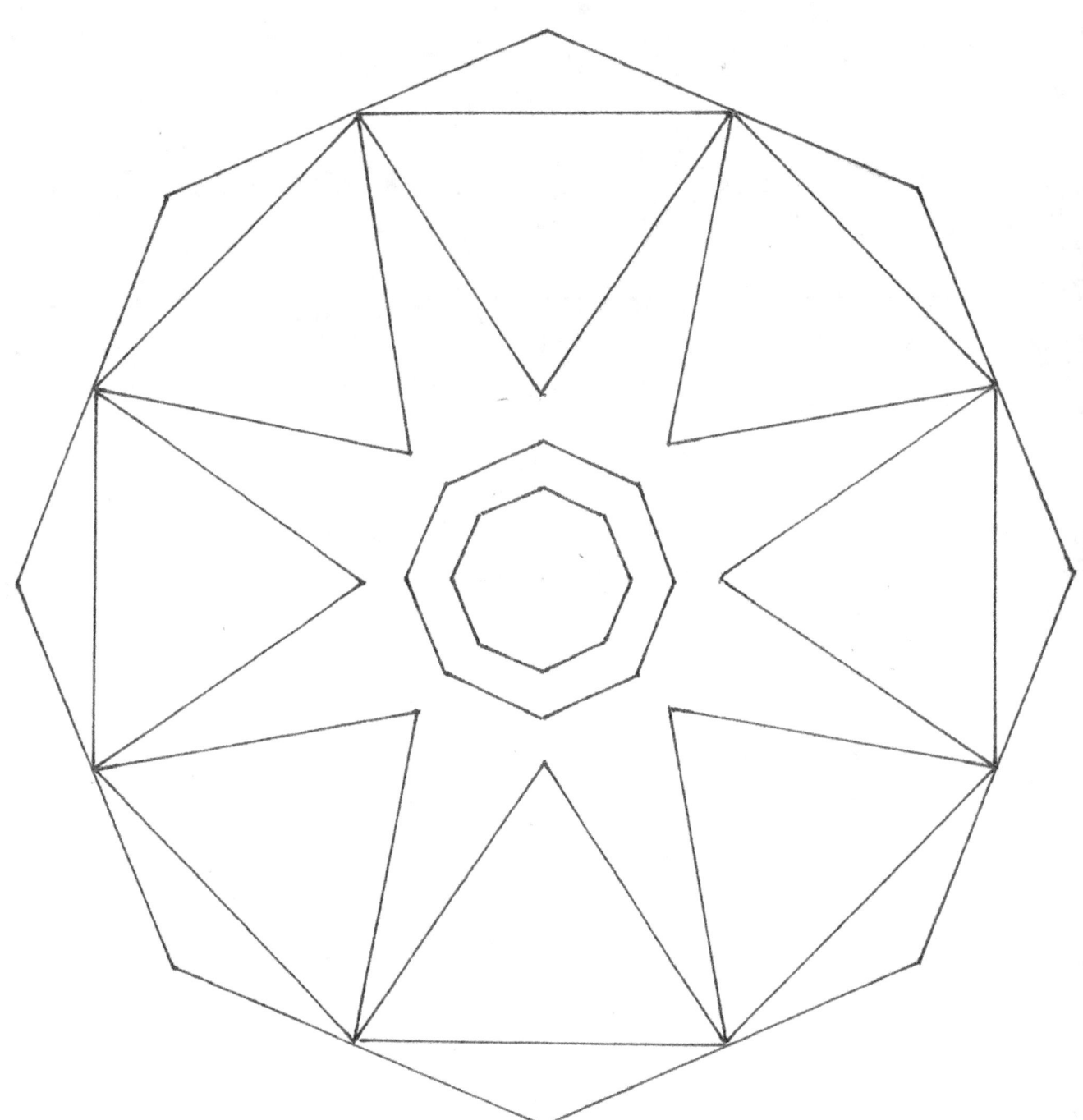

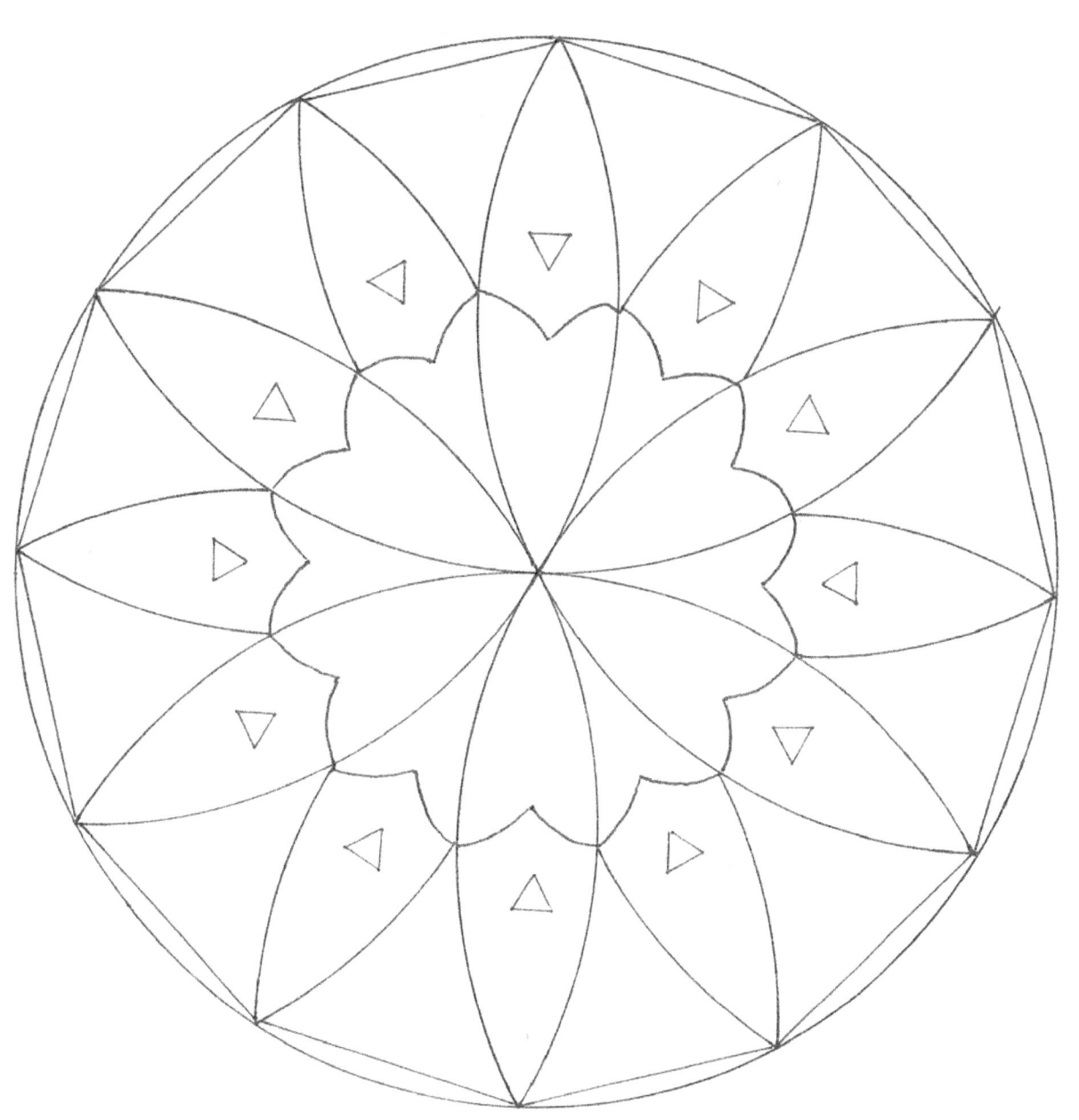

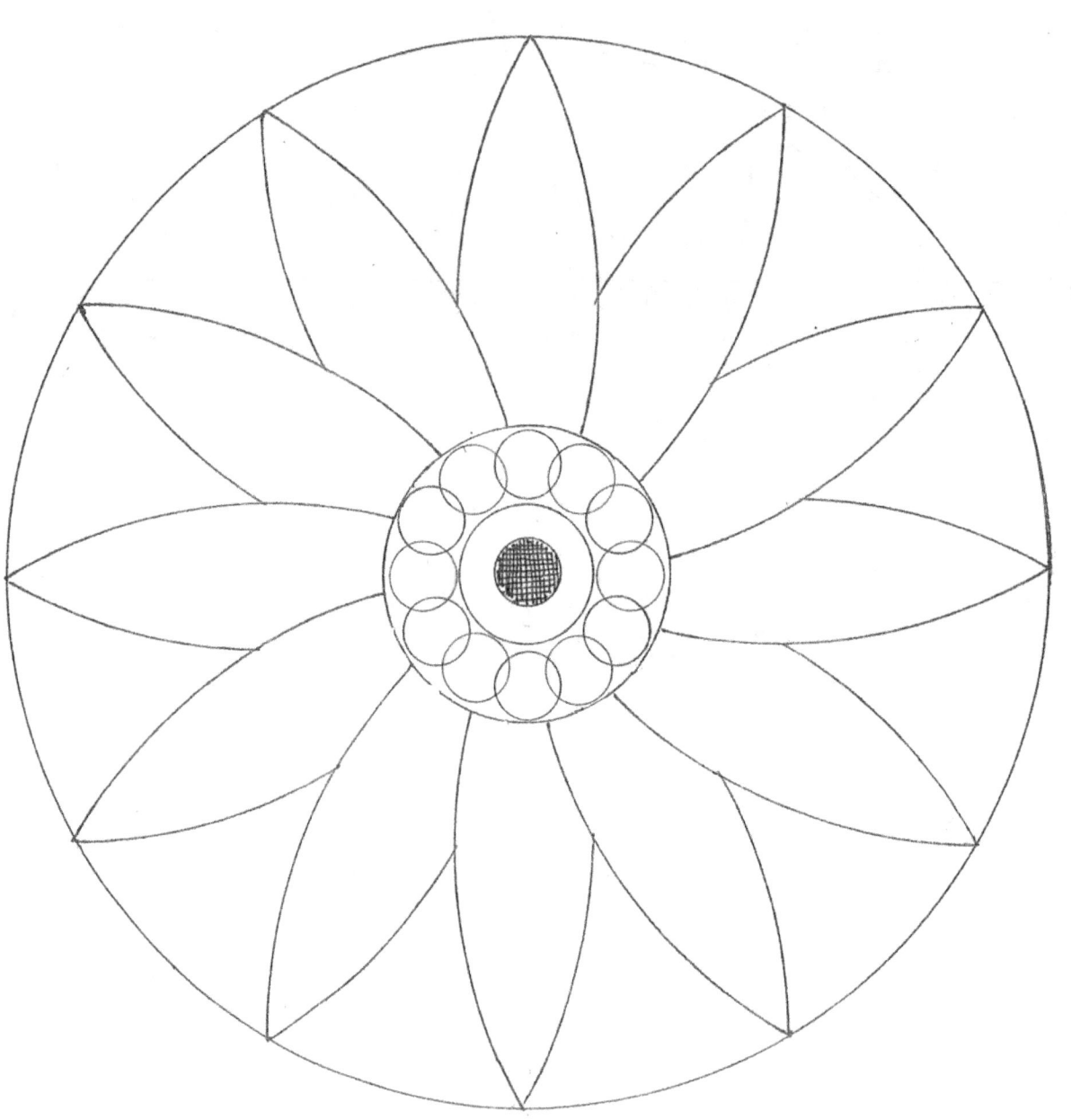

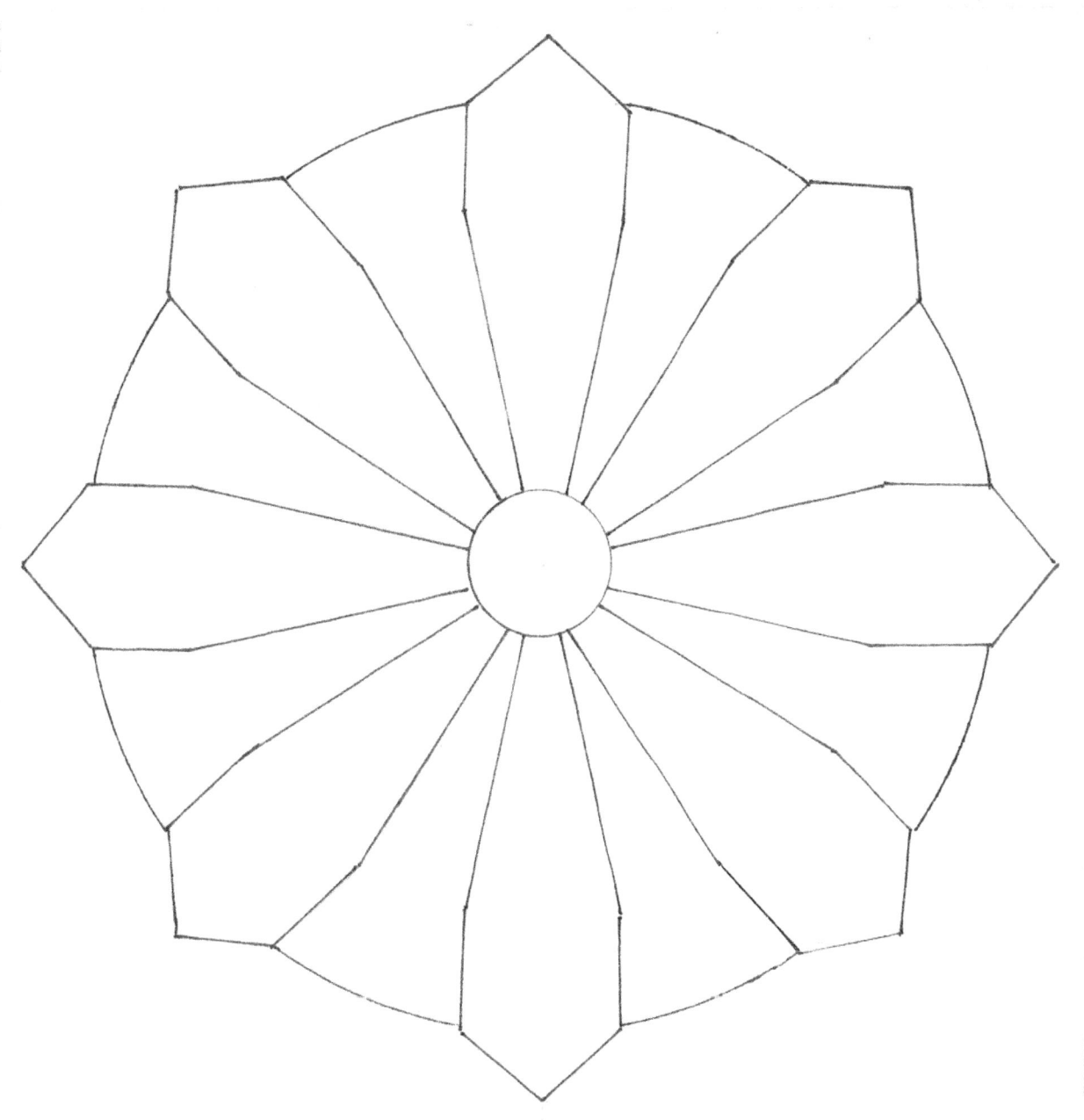

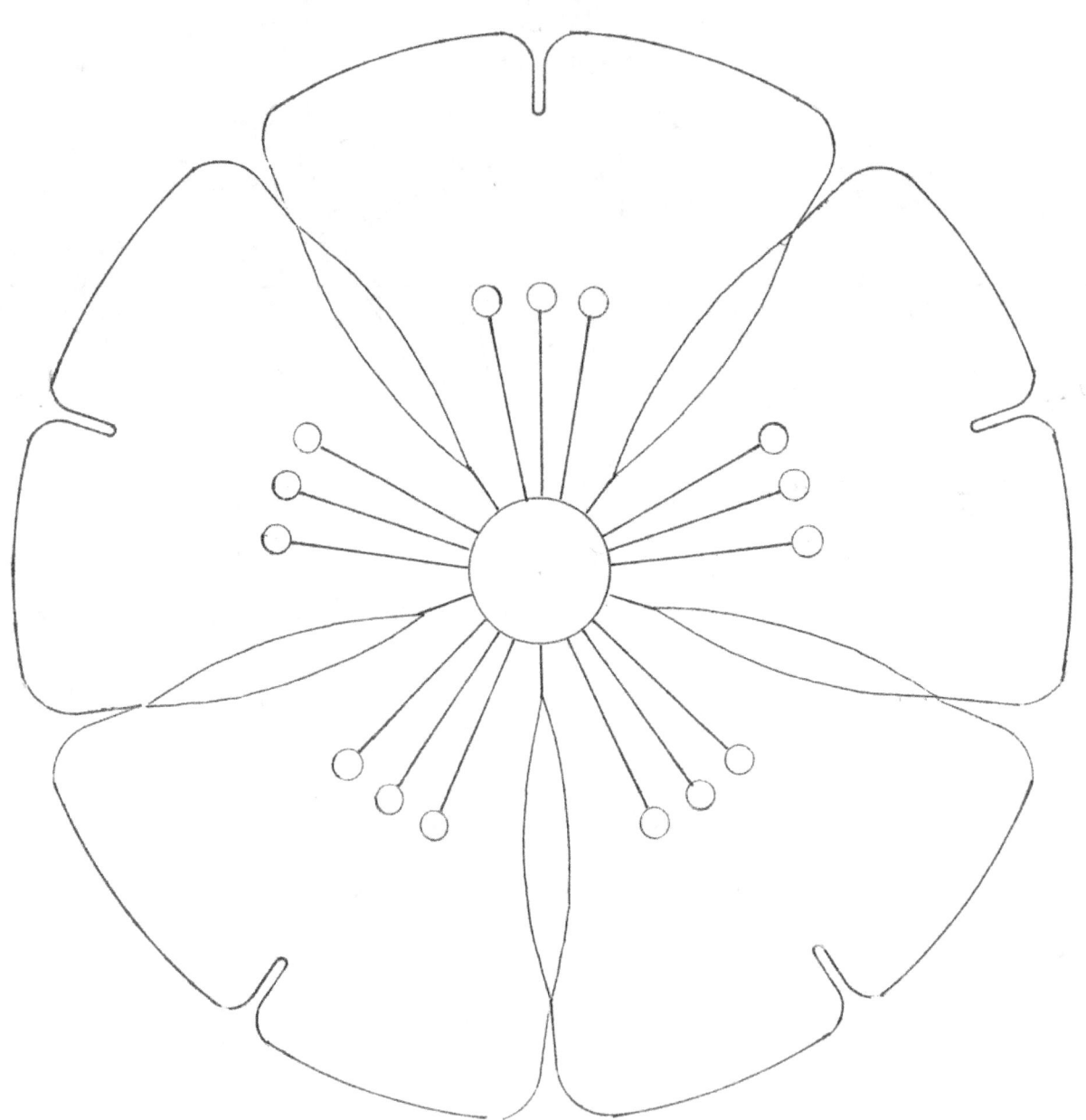

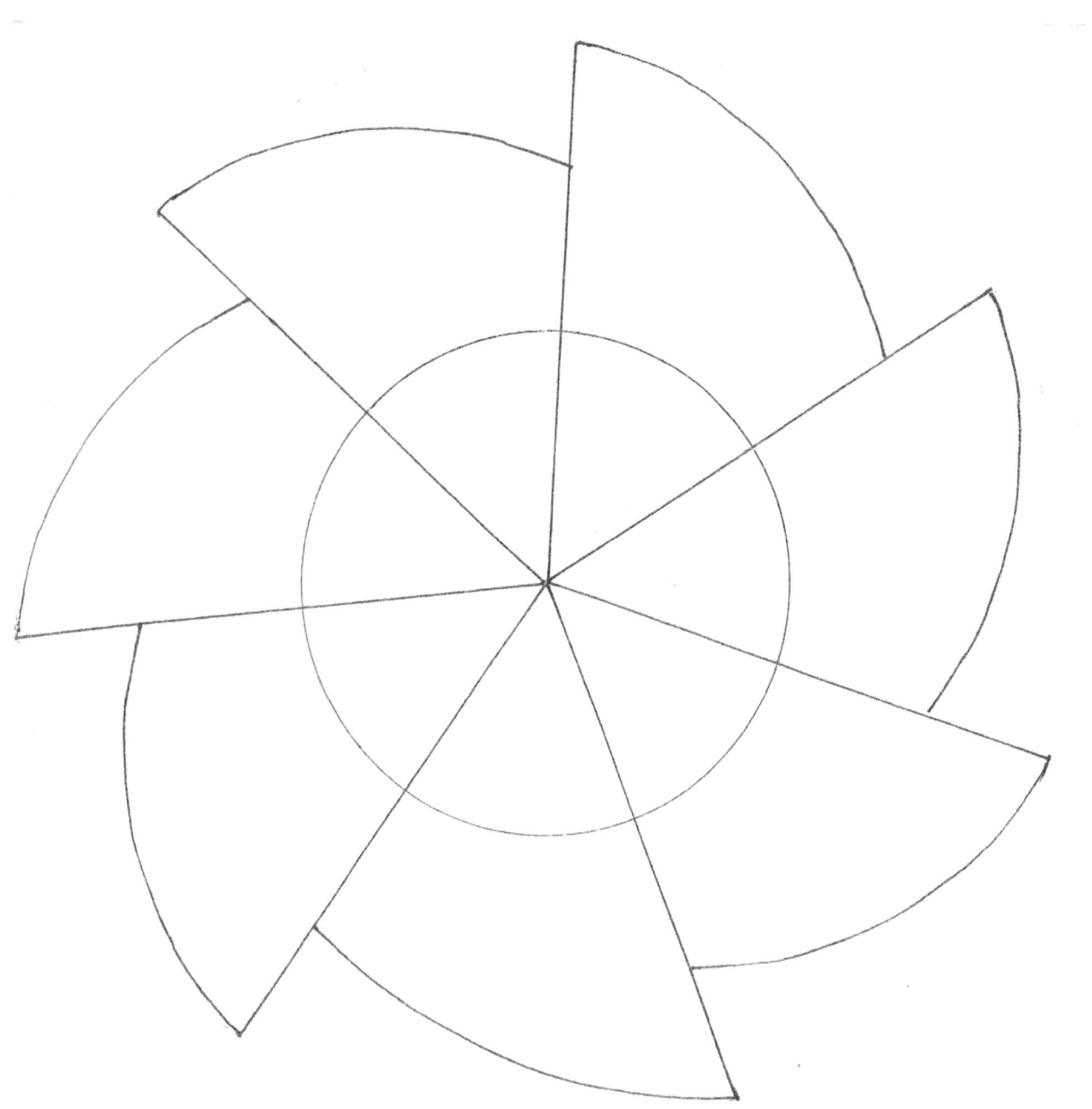

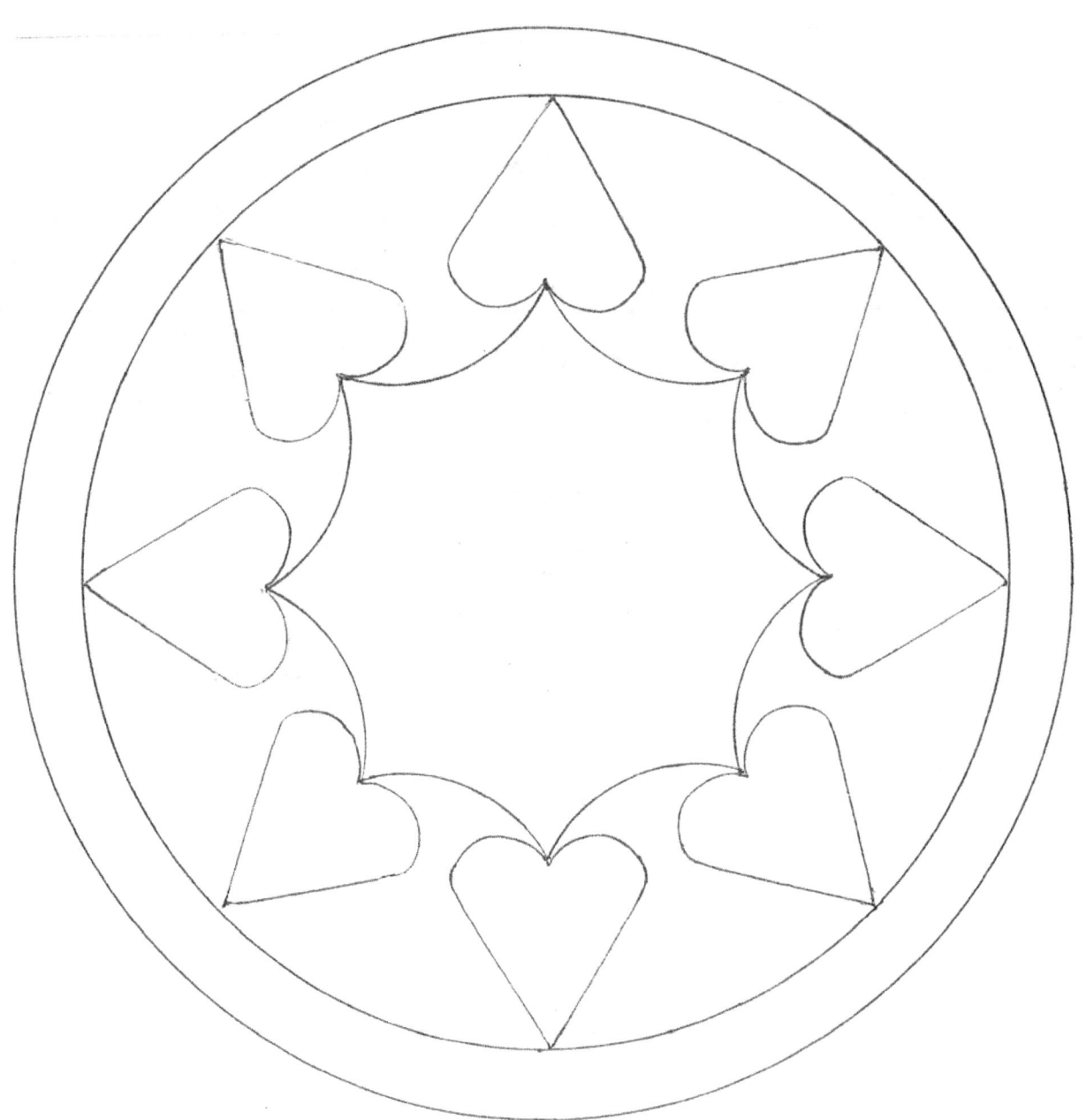

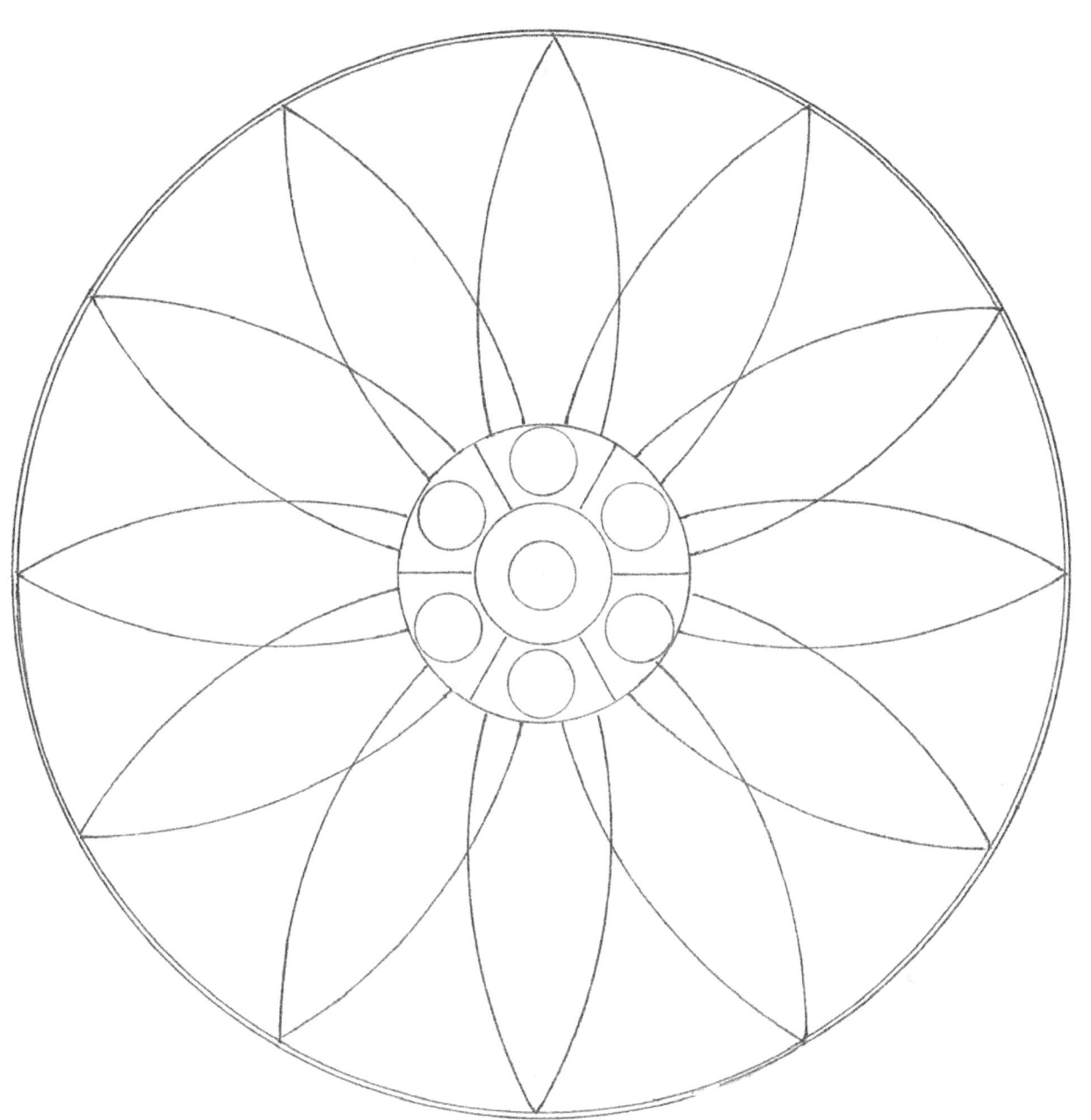

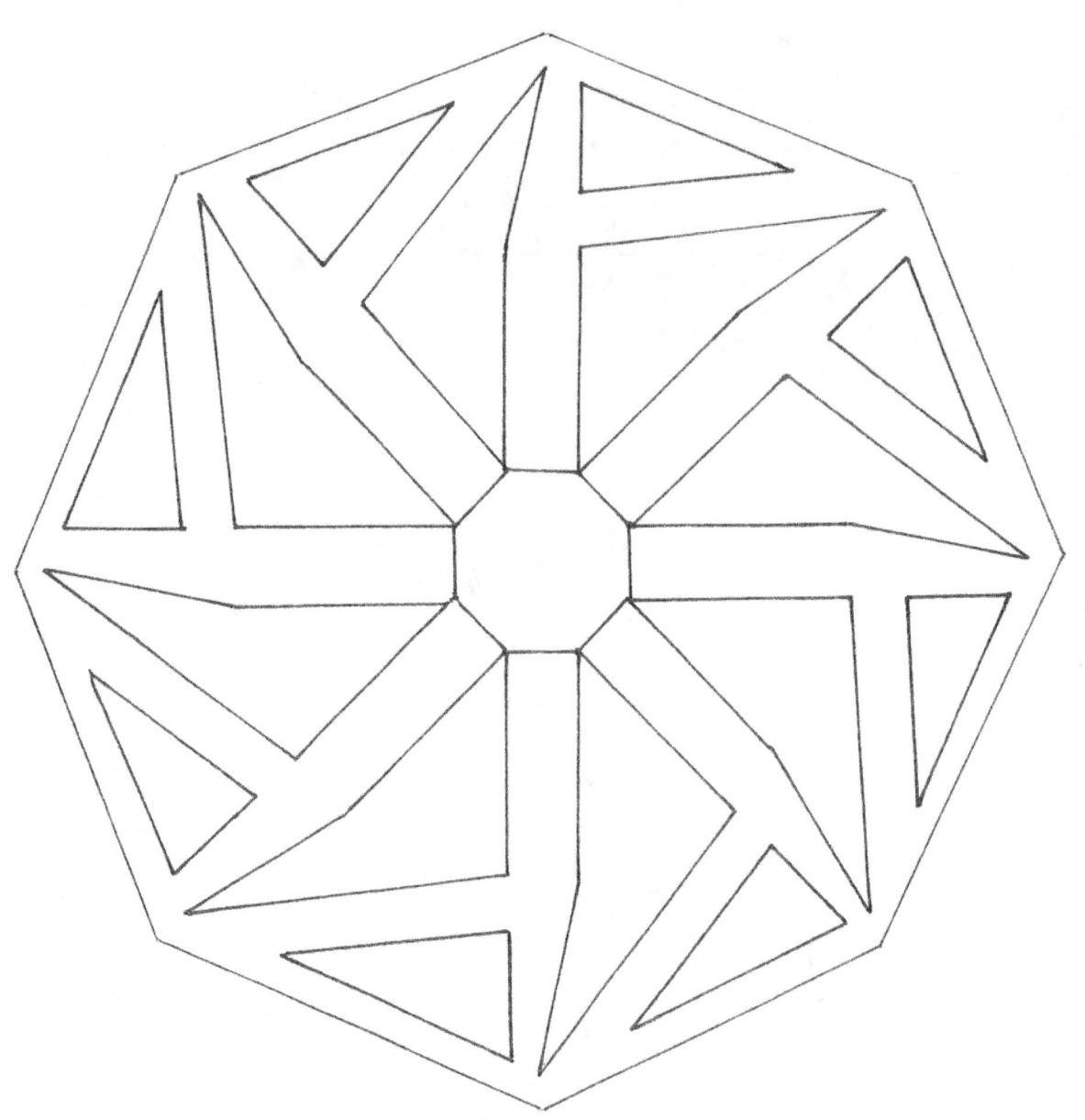

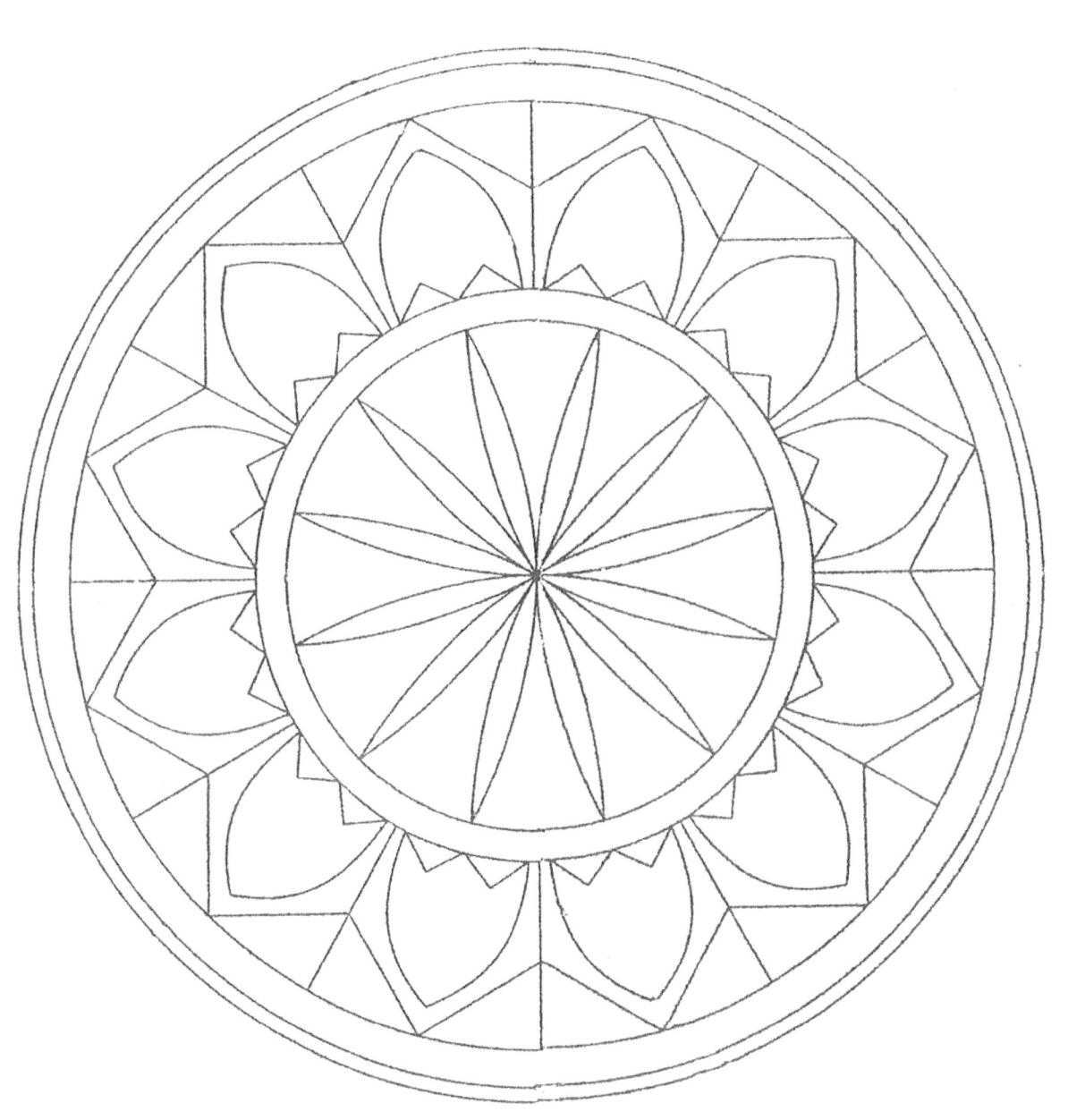

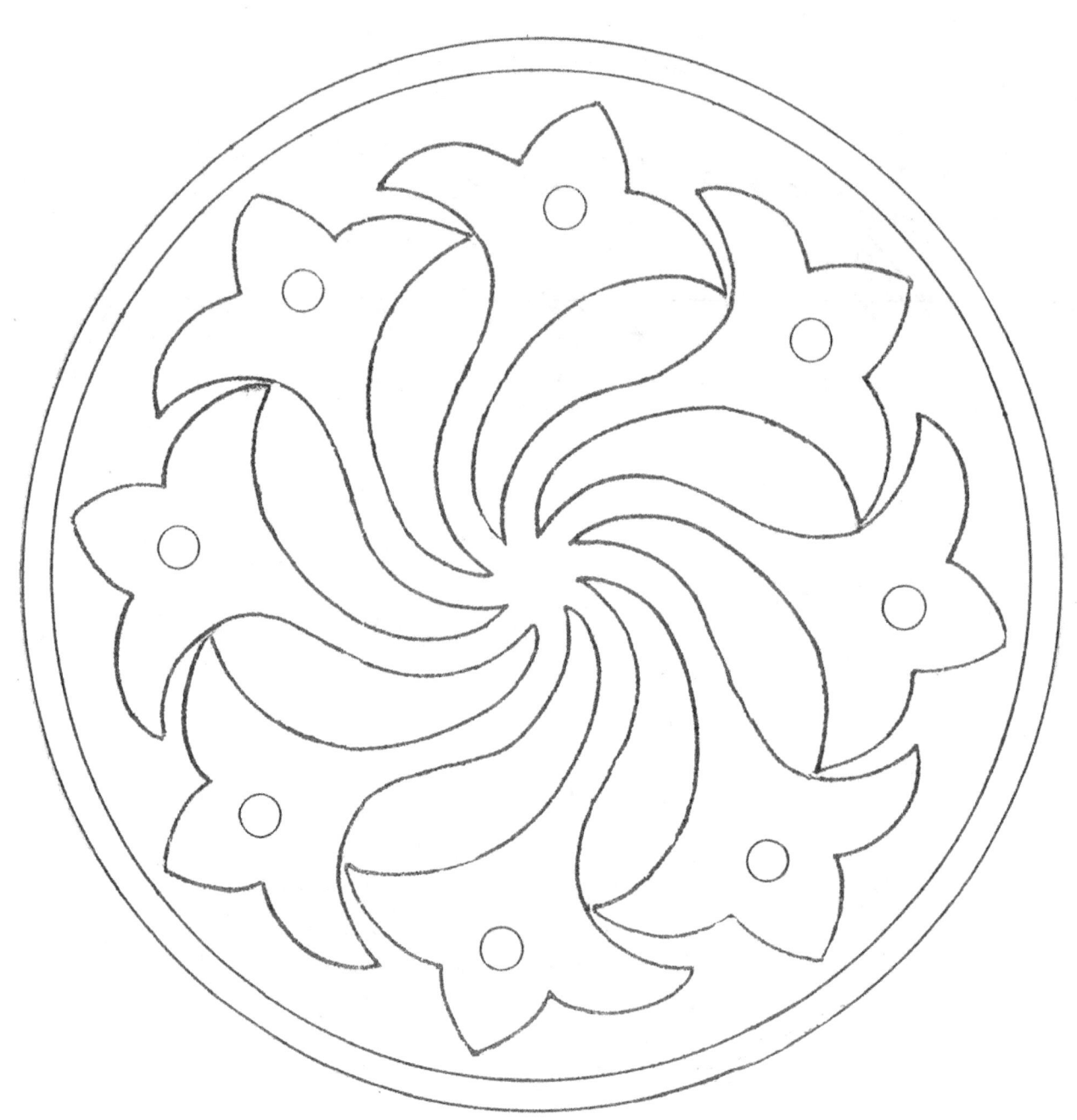

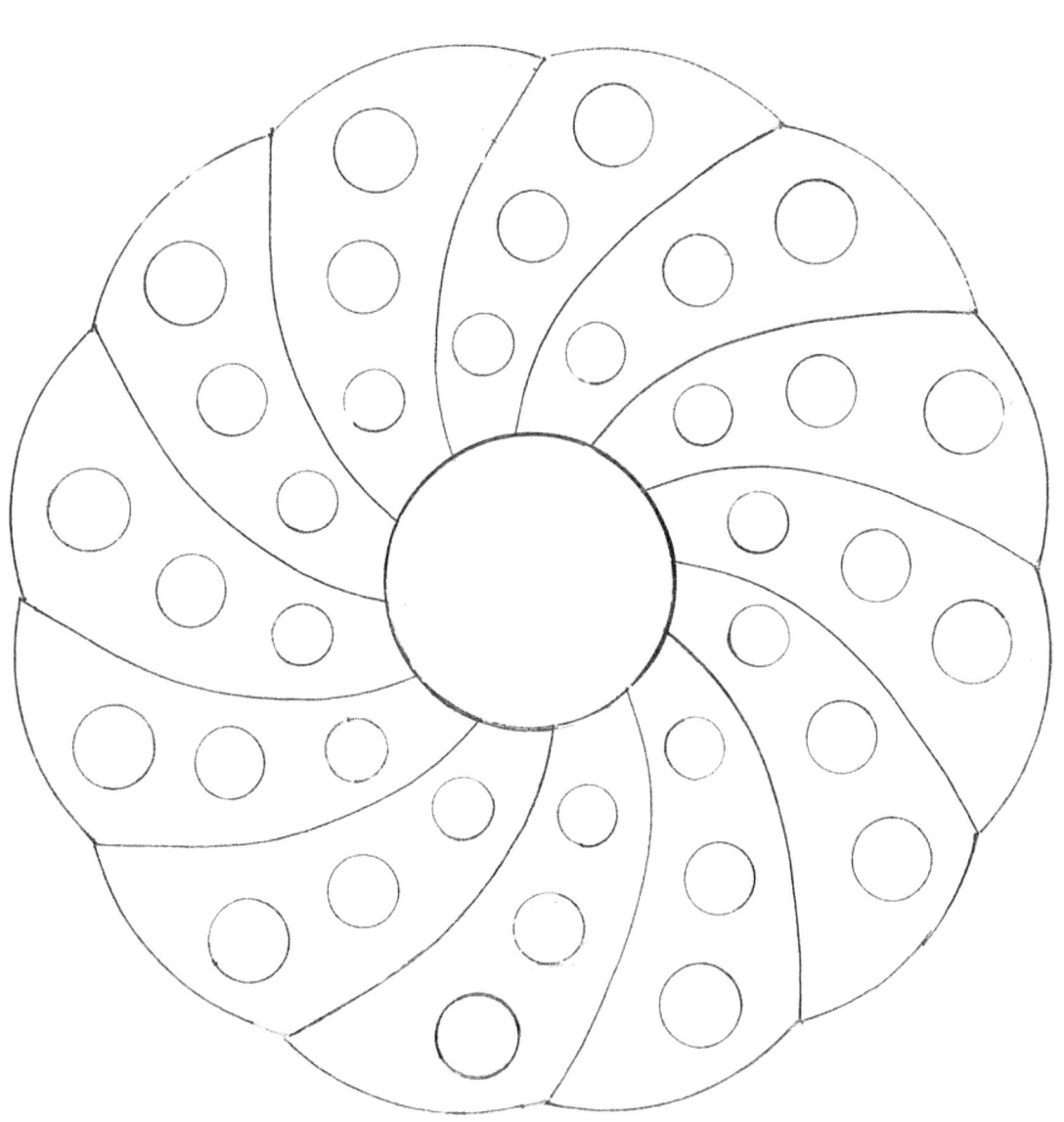

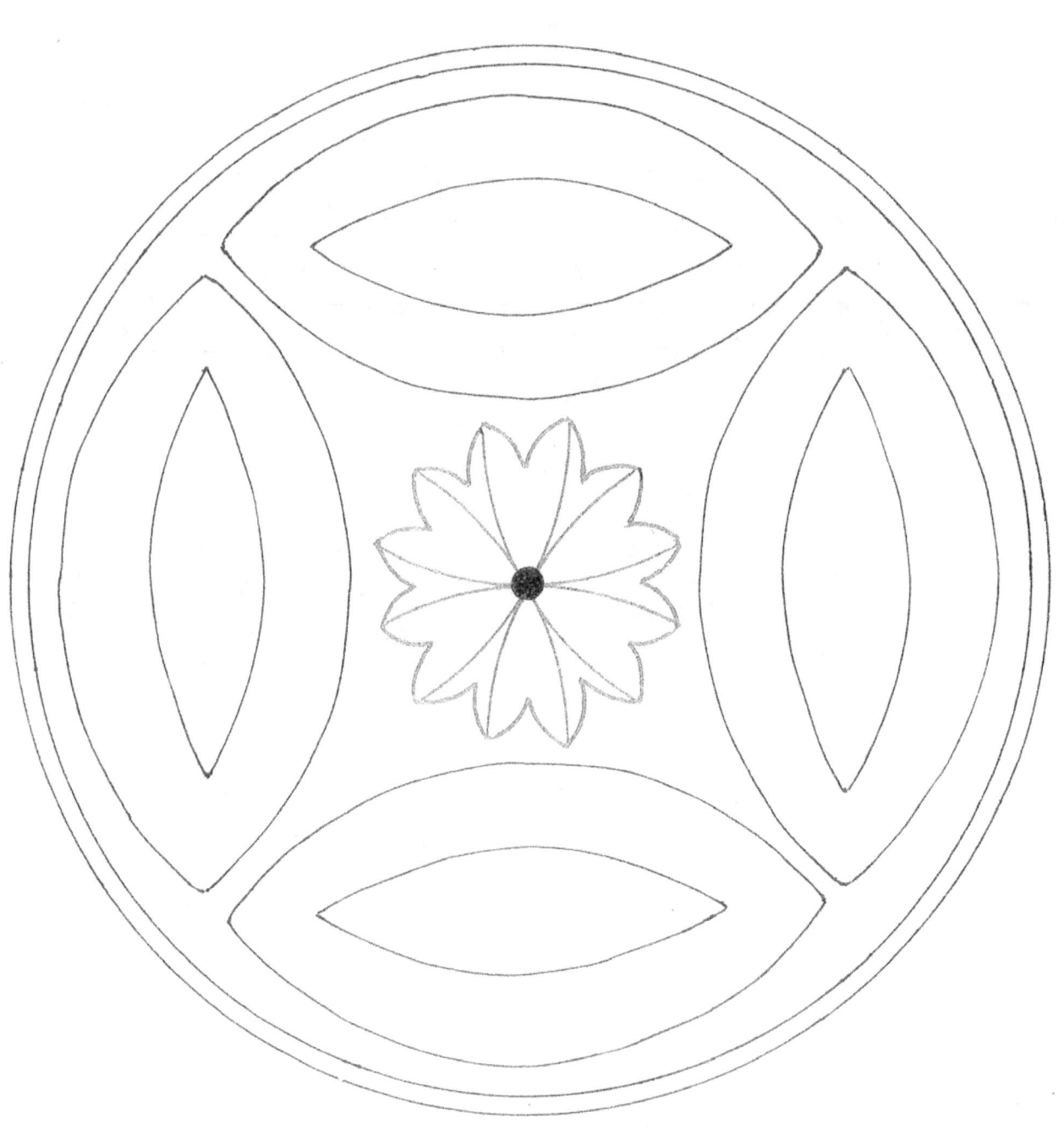

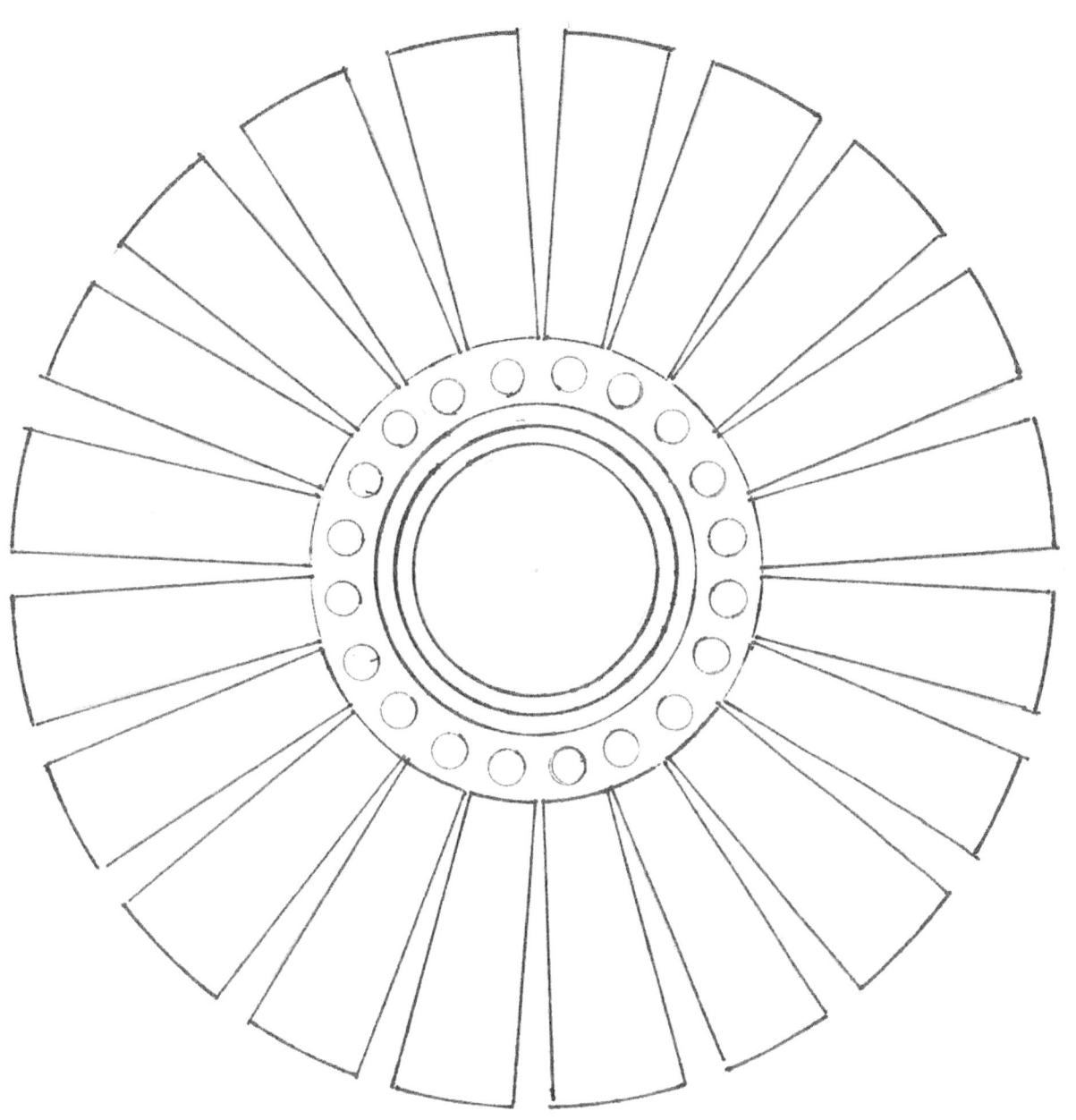

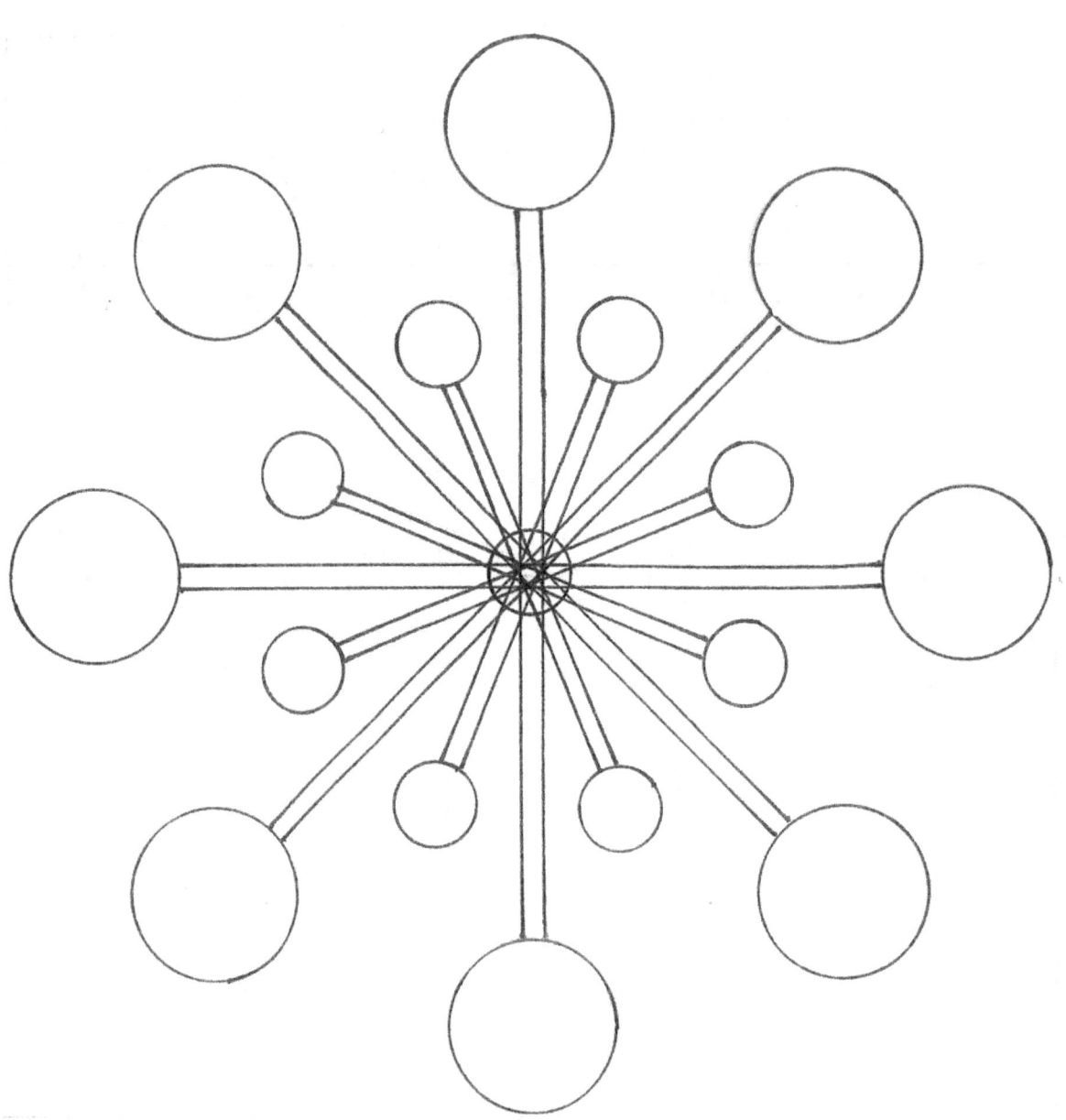

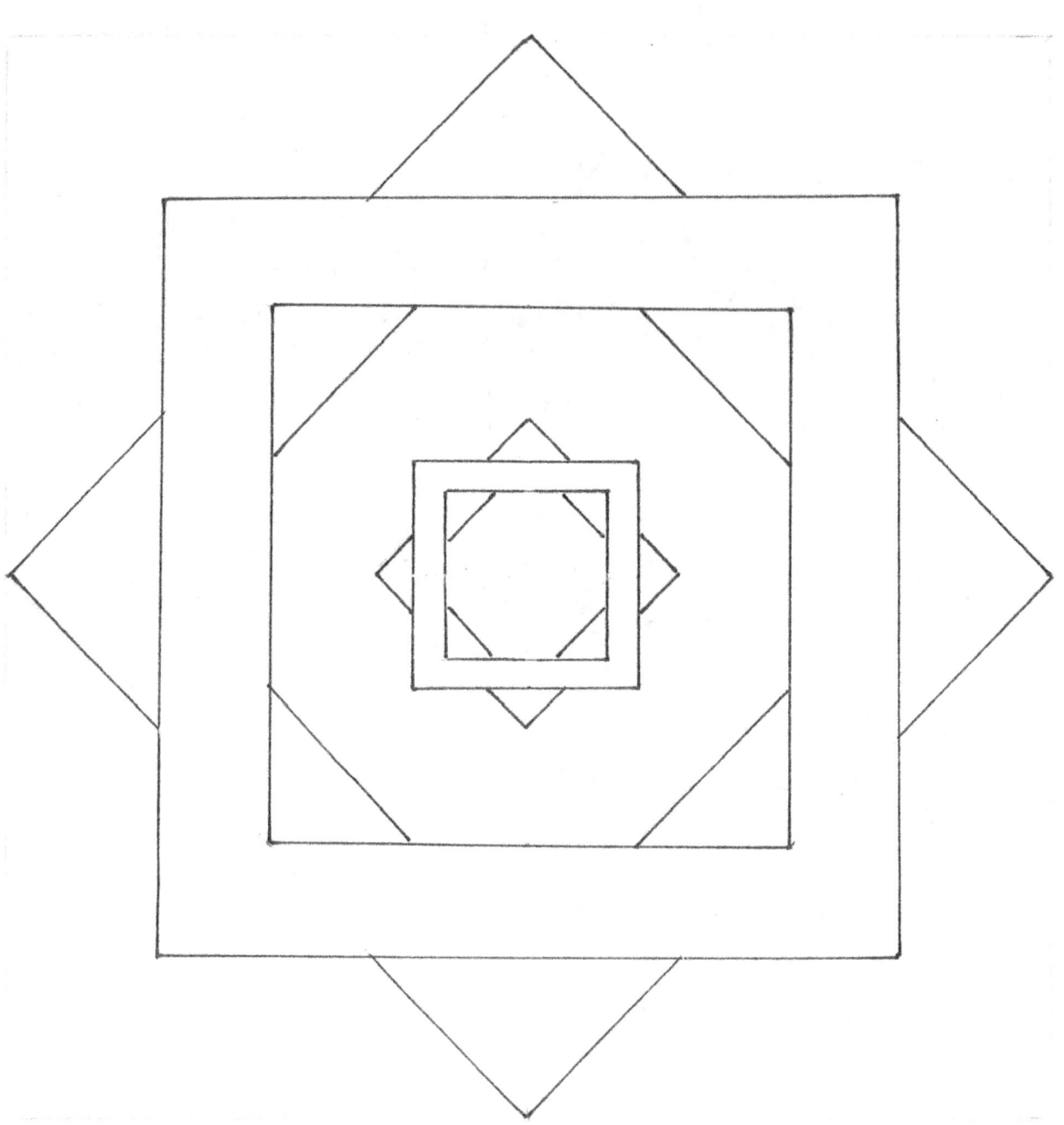

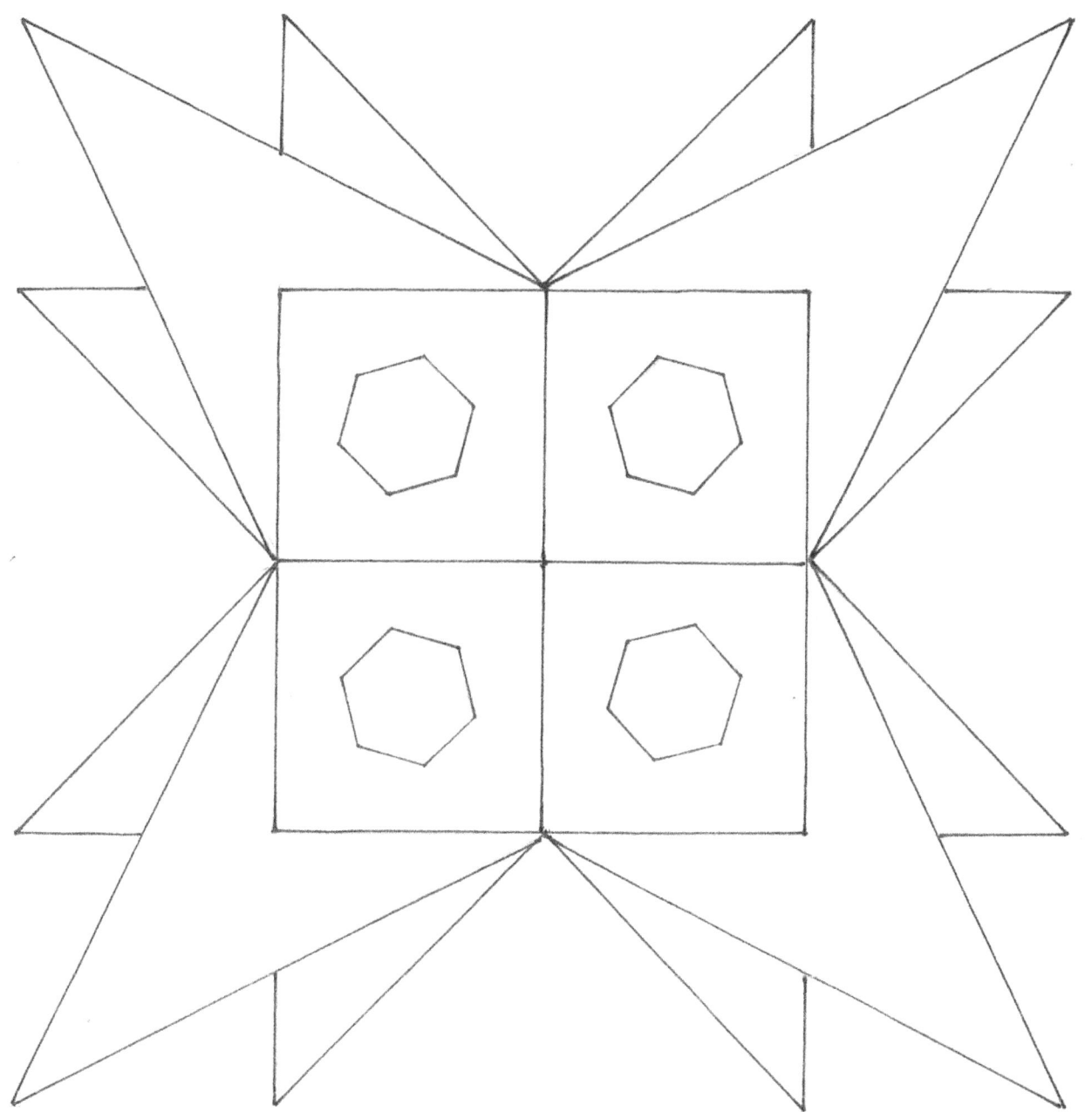

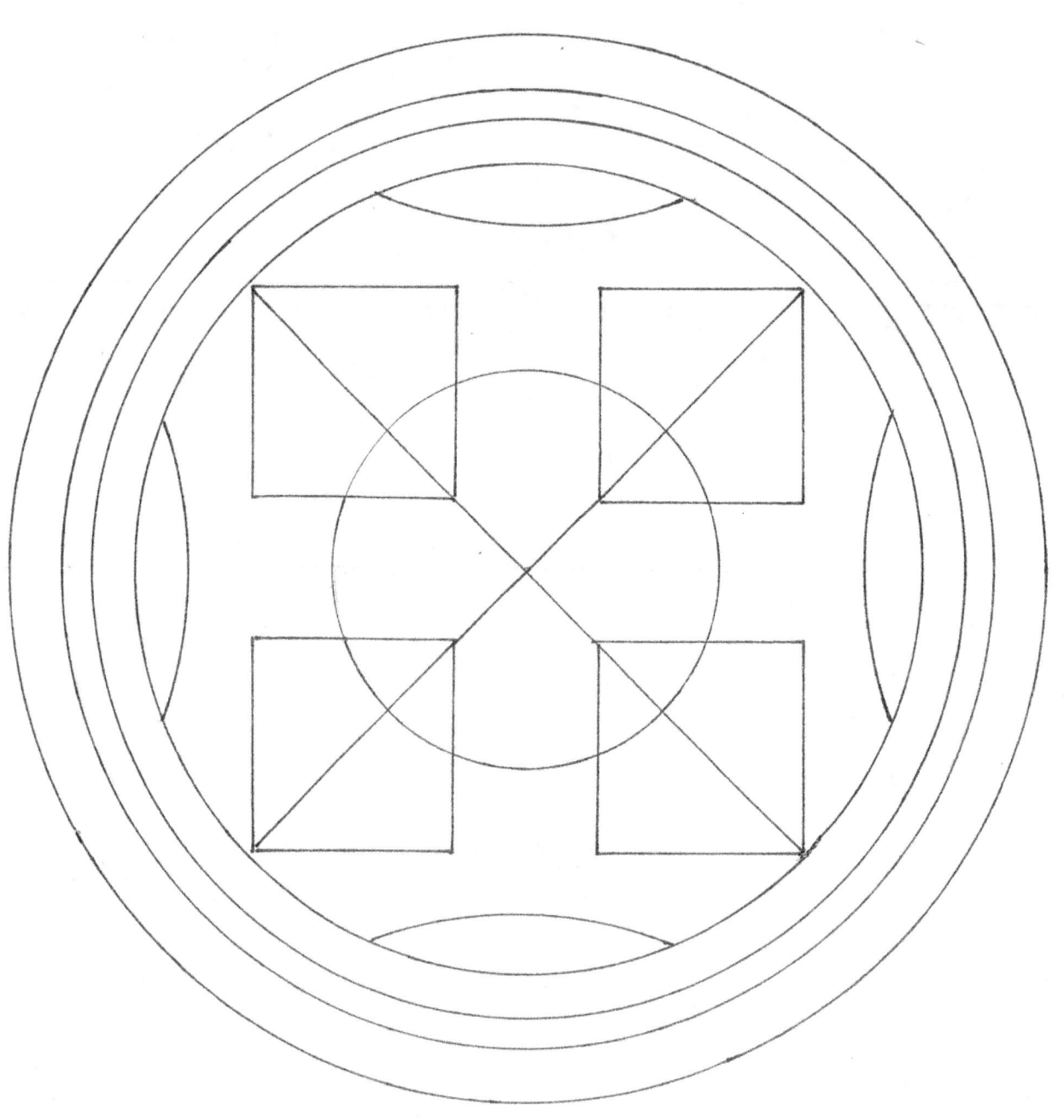

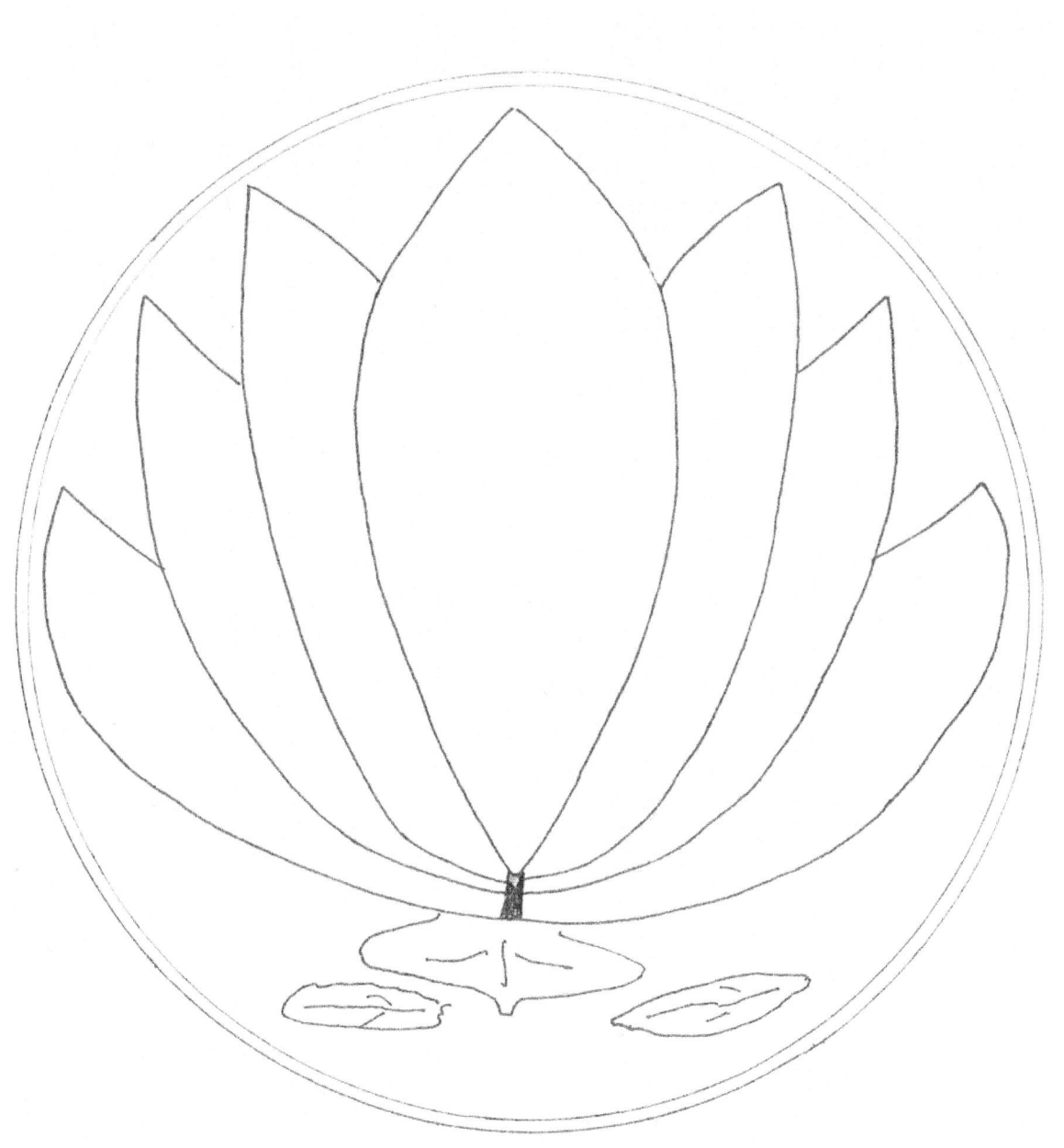

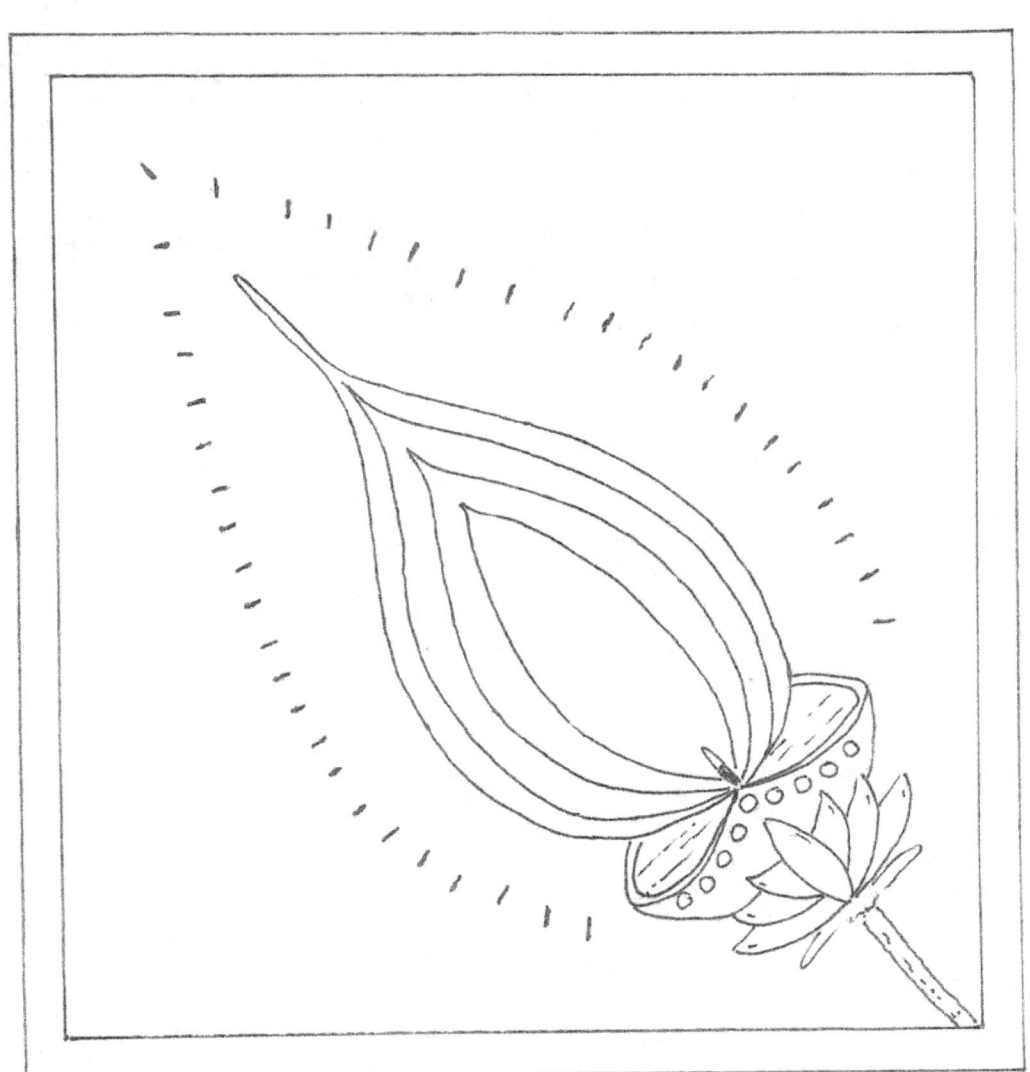

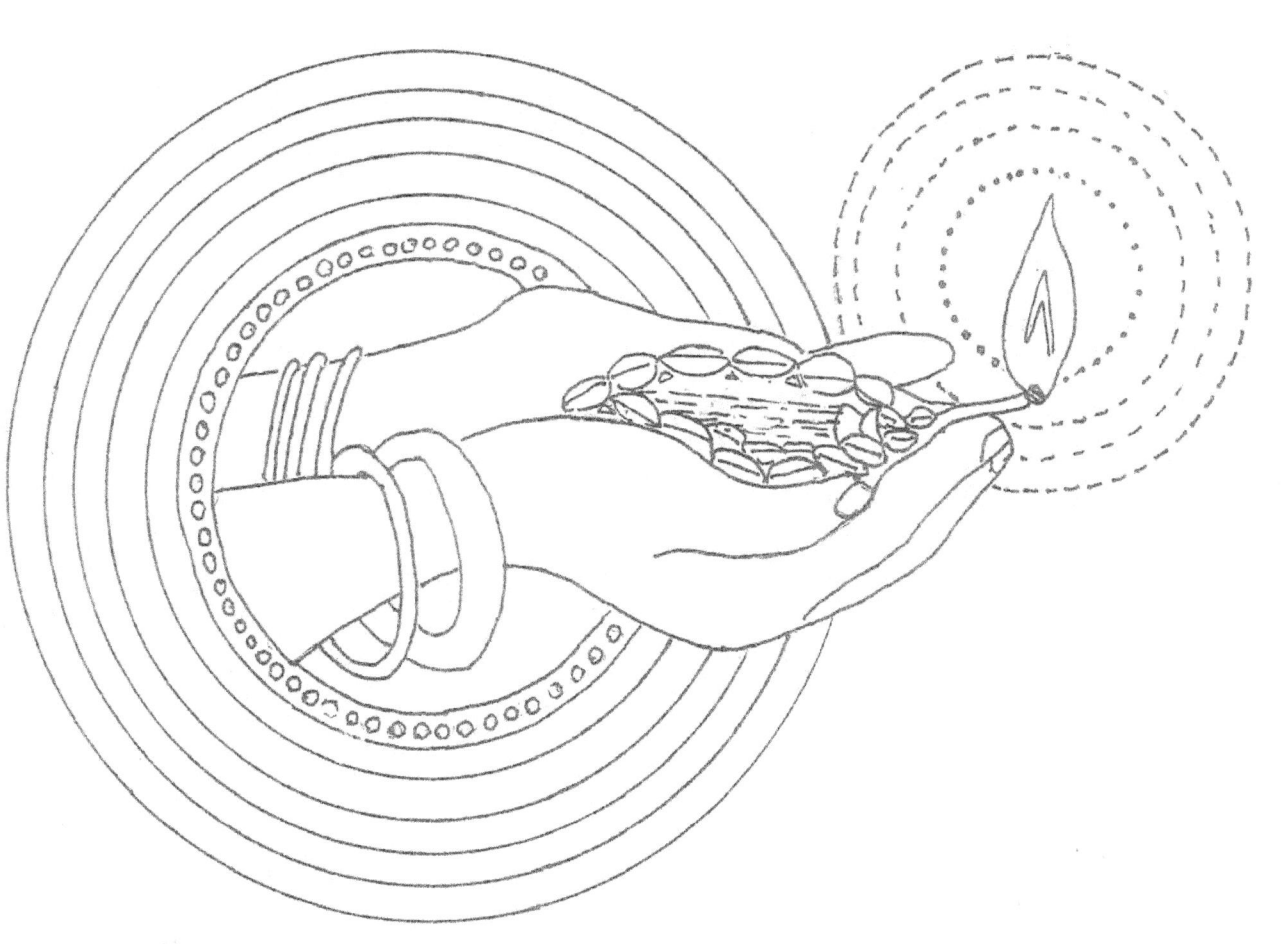

About this collection

This collection is a compilation of selected designs that have been hand drawn by the Author. They are intended to provide ideas and inspiration for drawing Rangoli. The patterns can be modified as needed. An outline of the pattern can be drawn onto the floor using a grid. Colors and other motifs are left to the artist to incorporate into their work as needed. It is intended that these patterns will help foster interest and creativity in creating rangoli.

About the Author

Mr Chandrakant R Patel operated a screen-printing business in Nairobi, Kenya for more than 30 years. Every year, he would design a colorful rangoli which was screen-printed as a sticker that could be easily applied to floors or walls. These were then distributed to family and friends. Over time, these became very popular and there was a high demand. The cover picture shows one of these designs. The collection in this book was drawn following his retirement, and these designs have not previously been printed.

C R Patel
3908 Tarrington Lane
Columbus, Ohio 43220
rangoli.patterns@gmail.com

October 2008

www.ingramcontent.com/pod-product-compliance
Lightning Source LLC
Chambersburg PA
CBHW081141170526
45165CB00008B/2753